THE ART OF COOKERY
MADE EASY AND REFINED

LECTOR HOUSE PUBLIC DOMAIN WORKS

This book is a result of an effort made by Lector House towards making a contribution to the preservation and repair of original classic literature. The original text is in the public domain in the United States of America, and possibly other countries depending upon their specific copyright laws.

In an attempt to preserve, improve and recreate the original content, certain conventional norms with regard to typographical mistakes, hyphenations, punctuations and/or other related subject matters, have been corrected upon our consideration. However, few such imperfections might not have been rectified as they were inherited and preserved from the original content to maintain the authenticity and construct, relevant to the work. The work might contain a few prior copyright references as well as page references which have been retained, wherever considered relevant to the part of the construct. We believe that this work holds historical, cultural and/or intellectual importance in the literary works community, therefore despite the oddities, we accounted the work for print as a part of our continuing effort towards preservation of literary work and our contribution towards the development of the society as a whole, driven by our beliefs.

We are grateful to our readers for putting their faith in us and accepting our imperfections with regard to preservation of the historical content. We shall strive hard to meet up to the expectations to improve further to provide an enriching reading experience.

Though, we conduct extensive research in ascertaining the status of copyright before redeveloping a version of the content, in rare cases, a classic work might be incorrectly marked as not-in-copyright. In such cases, if you are the copyright holder, then kindly contact us or write to us, and we shall get back to you with an immediate course of action.

HAPPY READING!

THE ART OF COOKERY MADE EASY AND REFINED

JOHN MOLLARD

ISBN: 978-93-89614-02-2

Published: 1802

LECTOR HOUSE LLP
E-MAIL: lectorpublishing@gmail.com

THE ART OF COOKERY MADE EASY AND REFINED;

COMPRISING
AMPLE DIRECTIONS FOR PREPARING EVERY ARTICLE
REQUISITE FOR FURNISHING THE TABLES
OF THE NOBLEMAN, GENTLEMAN,
AND TRADESMAN.

BY

JOHN MOLLARD, COOK;

Lately one of the Proprietors of Freemasons' Tavern, Great
Queen Street, Lincoln's Inn Fields; now removed to
Dover Street, Piccadilly, formerly THOMAS's.

SECOND EDITION.

1802.

PREFACE.

THE mode of cookery which the author of the following sheets has pursued for a series of years having obtained the most distinguished approbation of the public, has induced him to commit his practice to paper; in doing which, a deviation has been made from the usual introductory methods of other treatises of the kind, in omitting to give particular directions for the choice of fish, meats, poultry, and vegetables, and at what times they respectively might be in season, &c. &c. the author conceiving the simpler method to be the most acceptable: and, therefore, as actual knowledge must ever supersede written forms, he would advise a frequent attendance at the different markets, fully assured that experience will convey greater instruction in marketing than all the theories which could be advanced. There are, nevertheless, some useful observations interspersed in the course of the work for that purpose; the author having confined himself chiefly to the practical part of cookery; he has also given some directions in a branch of the confectionary business: in both of which it has been his constant endeavour that they might be rendered as simple and easy as possible, and that economy might pervade the whole.

The receipts are written for the least possible quantities in the different made-dishes and sauces, it being a frequent error in most of the books that they are too expensive and too long; by which means the art has been rendered intricate in the extreme, both in theory and practice.

Independent, also, of a close adherence to any given rules, there are other qualities essential to the completion of a thorough cook; such as, an acute taste, a fertile invention, and a rigid attention to cleanliness.

The preceding hints and subsequent directions, it is hoped, will prove fully adequate to perfection in cookery; the work being entirely divested of the many useless receipts from other professions, (which have been uniformly introduced in books of the like nature,) and nothing inserted but what has an immediate reference to the art itself.

There is prefixed a Bill of Fare for each month in the year, as a specimen of the seasons, which may be altered as judgment directs. There is annexed, also, at the end of the volume, an Index, by which, from the first letter or word of the different articles, will be found their respective receipts.

February 2d, 1802.

CONTENTS

Page

THE ART OF COOKERY

For
JANUARY.
1st Course
Soup Santé
Small Ham
Tendlons Veal white
Slices Crimp'd Cod
Mashd Jacks Potatoes
Rump Beef glaz'd wth Harricott
Brocoli
Whitings Broild
Pullet wth Oyster Sauce
Raizd Lamb Pies
Mock'd Turtle
2d Course
Wood Cocks Roast.
Scollop Shells
Stew'd Mushrooms
Apple Fritters
Truffle
Shellfish in an Ornamented Bat
Jelly
Fry'd Puffs wth Sweetmeats
Stew'd Cardoons
Omlett wth Cullis
Partridges Roast.
Neele Sc. Strand

For
JANUARY.

1st. Course

Soup
Santé

Small Ham

Tendlons Veal
white

Slises
Crimp'd Cod

M^{d.} & whole
Potatoes

Rump Beef glaiz^d
wth. Harricott

Brocoli

Whitings
Broil'd

Pullet w^{th.}
Oyster Sauce

Raiz'd Lamb Pies

Mock'd Turtle

2^{d.} Course

Wood Cocks
Roast.

Scollop
Shells

Stew'd
Mushrooms

Apple Fritters

Shellfish
in an
Ornamented
Ba^{s.}

Triffle

Jelly

Fry'd Puffs
w^{th.}

Sweetmeats

Omlett
w^{th.}
Cullis

Stew'd
Cardoons

Partridges
Roast.

FEBRUARY.

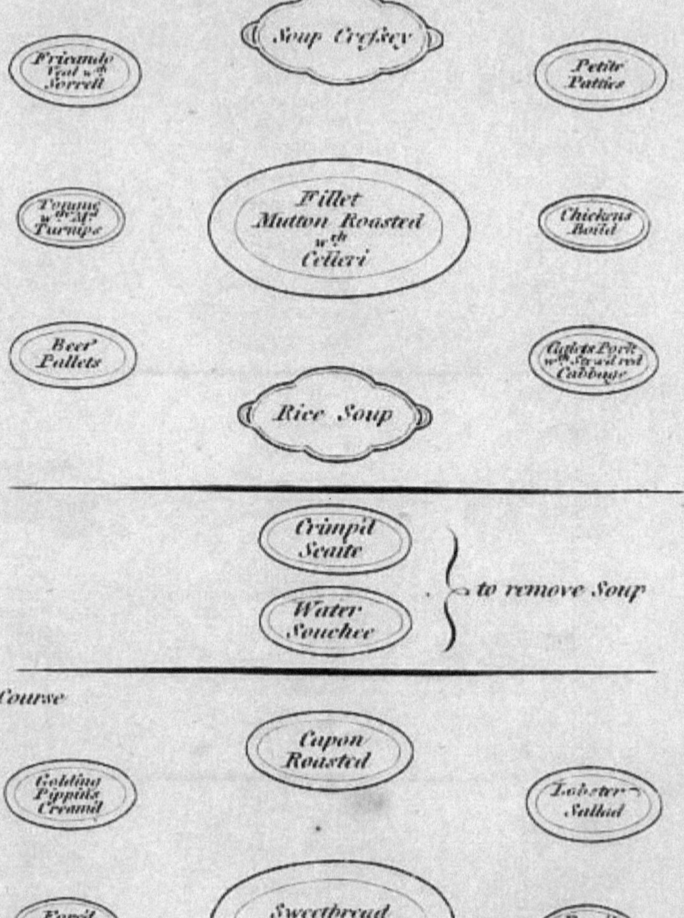

Neele Sc. Strand

FEBRUARY.

1ˢᵗ· Course

Frieandd Veal wᵗʰ· Sorrell	*Soup Cressey*	*Petite Patties*
Tongue wᵗʰ· Mᵈ· Turnips	*Fillet Mutton Roasted wᵗʰ· Celleri*	*Chickens Boil'd*
Beef Pallets	*Rice Soup*	*Cutlets Pork wᵗʰ· Stew'd red Cabbage*
	Crimp'd Seaite	
		to remove Soup
	Water Soucher	

2ᵈ· Course

Golding Pippins Cream'd	*Capon Roasted*	*Lobster Sallad*
Forc'd Asparagus	*Sweetbread Roast*	*Forc'd French Beans*
Slic'd Brawn	*Teal Roast*	*Ribband Blancmange*

MARCH.

1.st Course

Soup
and Boullie

Soles Frey'd
and Boild

Crimp'd Cods
Head

Soup ala Reine

2.d Course

Fillet Pork
Roast.

Harricott
or
Begetables

Potatoes
Mashd

French Pie

Mashd
Turnips

Veal Olives

Leg Lamb
and
Spinach

3.d Course

Turkey Roast

Marbree
Jelly

Tourte

Brocoli
ala Sauce

Pick'd Crabb

Sausages

Pyrimid
of Paste

Pippins
wth Rice

Large Pidgeons
Roast.

MARCH.

1^(st.) Course

*Soup
and Boullie*

*Soles Fry'd
and Boild*

*Crimp'd Cods
Head*

Soup ala Reine

2^(d.) Course

Harricott of Begetables	*Fillet Pork Roast.*	*Potatoes Mash'd*
	French Pie	
Mash'd Turnips	*Leg Lamb and Spinach*	*Veal Olives*

3^(d.) Course

Marbree Jelly	*Turkey Roast.*	*Tourte*
Brocoli ala Sauce	*Pick'd Crabb*	*Sausages*
Pyrimid of Paste	*Large Pidgeons Roast.*	*Pippins w^(th.) Rice*

APRIL.

1st Course
Mock'd Turtle
Tongue Boil'd &c.
Chicken w.th Sweetbreads White
Sallad
Beef Forc'd and Roasted w.th Oy.r Sauce
Rice
Currie
Vermiceli Soup
Cutlets Lamb
Crimp'd Salmon & Fry'd Smelts
Stew'd Tench
to remove Soup
2d Course
Levrett Roast
Apricot tart w.th Curramel
Dutch Blancmange
Stew'd Cellery
Prawnes
Mushrooms Broil'd
Almond Cake
Apple Tart
Ducklings Roast.

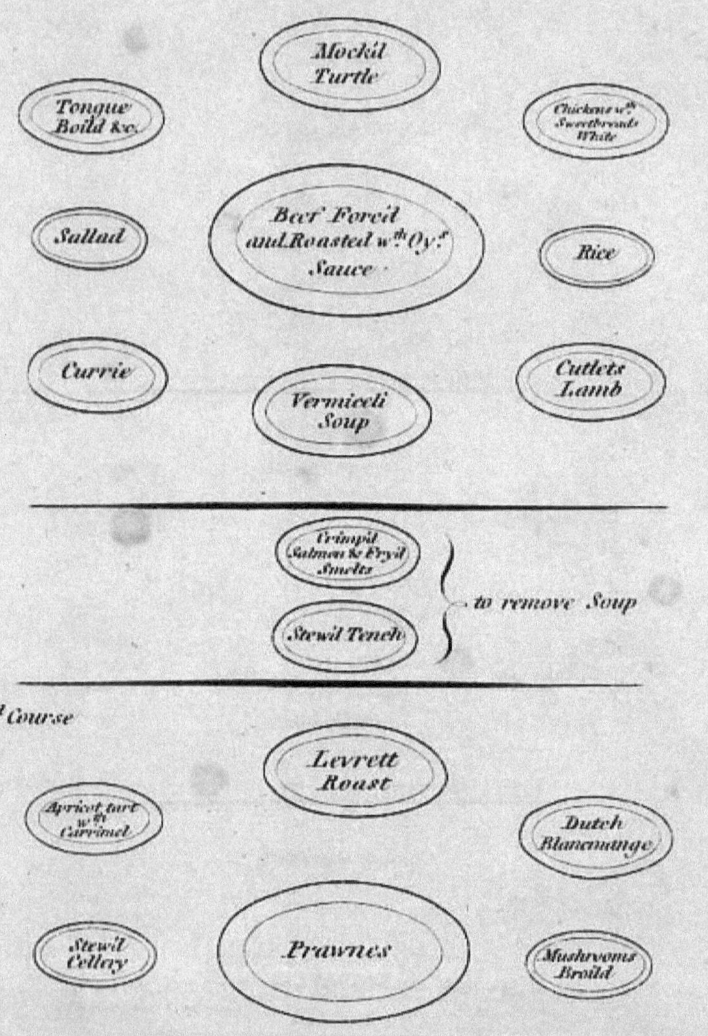

APRIL.

1ˢᵗ· Course

Tongue Boild &c.	*Mock'd Turtle*	*Chickens wᵗʰ· Sweetbreads White*
Sallad	*Beef Forc'd and Roasted wᵗʰ· Oyˢ· Sauce*	*Rice*
Currie	*Vermiceli Soup*	*Cutlets Lamb*
	Crimp'd Salmon & Fry'd Smelts	*to remove Soup*
	Stew'd Tench	

2ᵈ· Course

Apricot tart wᵗʰ· Carrimel	*Levrett Roast*	*Dutch Blancmange*
Stew'd Cellery	*Prawnes*	*Mushrooms Broild*
Almond Cake	*Ducklings Roast.*	*Apple Tart*

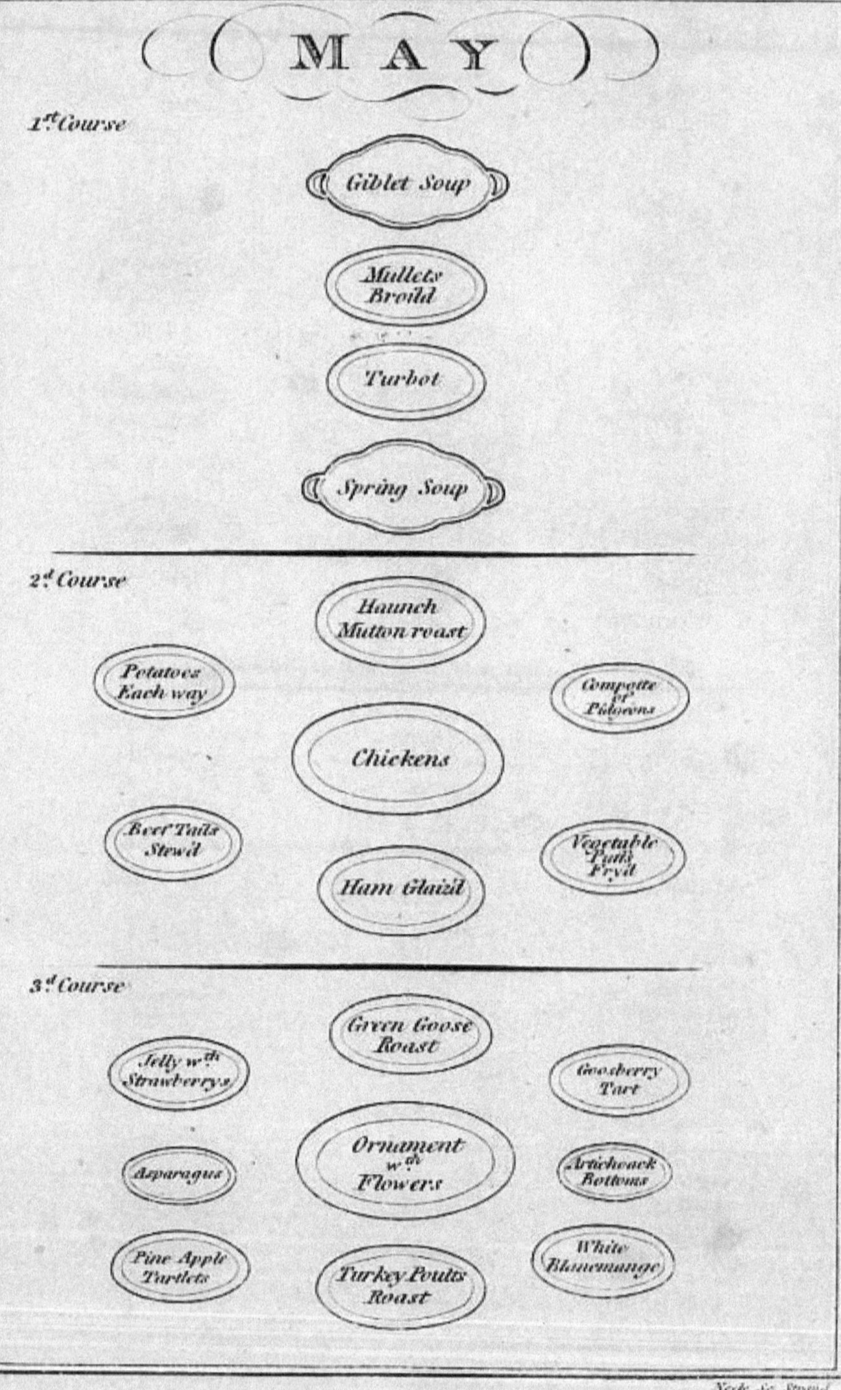

MAY
1st Course
Giblet Soup
Mullets Broild
Turbot
Spring Soup
2d Course
Haunch Mutton roast
Potatoes Each way
Compotte or Pidgeons
Chickens
Beet Tails Stewd
Vegetable Puffs Fryd
Ham Glaizd
3d Course
Green Goose Roast
Jelly wth Strawberrys
Goosberry Tart
Asparagus
Ornament wth Flowers
Artichoack Bottoms
Pine Apple Tartlets
Turkey Poults Roast
White Blanemange
Neele Sc. Strand

MAY.

1st. Course

Giblet Soup
Mullets
Broild
Turbot
Spring Soup

2^{d.} Course

	Haunch	
	Mutton roast	*Compotte*
Potatoes		*of*
Each way		*Pidgeons*
	Chickens	
Beef Tails		*Vegetable*
Stew'd		*Puffs*
	Ham Glaiz'd	*Fry'd*

3^{d.} Course

Jelly w^{th.}	*Green Goose*	
Strawberrys	*Roast*	*Goosberry Tart*
	Ornament	*Artichoack*
Asparagus	*w^{th.}*	*Bottoms*
	Flowers	
Pine Apple	*Turkey Poults*	*White*
Tartlets	*Roast*	*Blancmange*

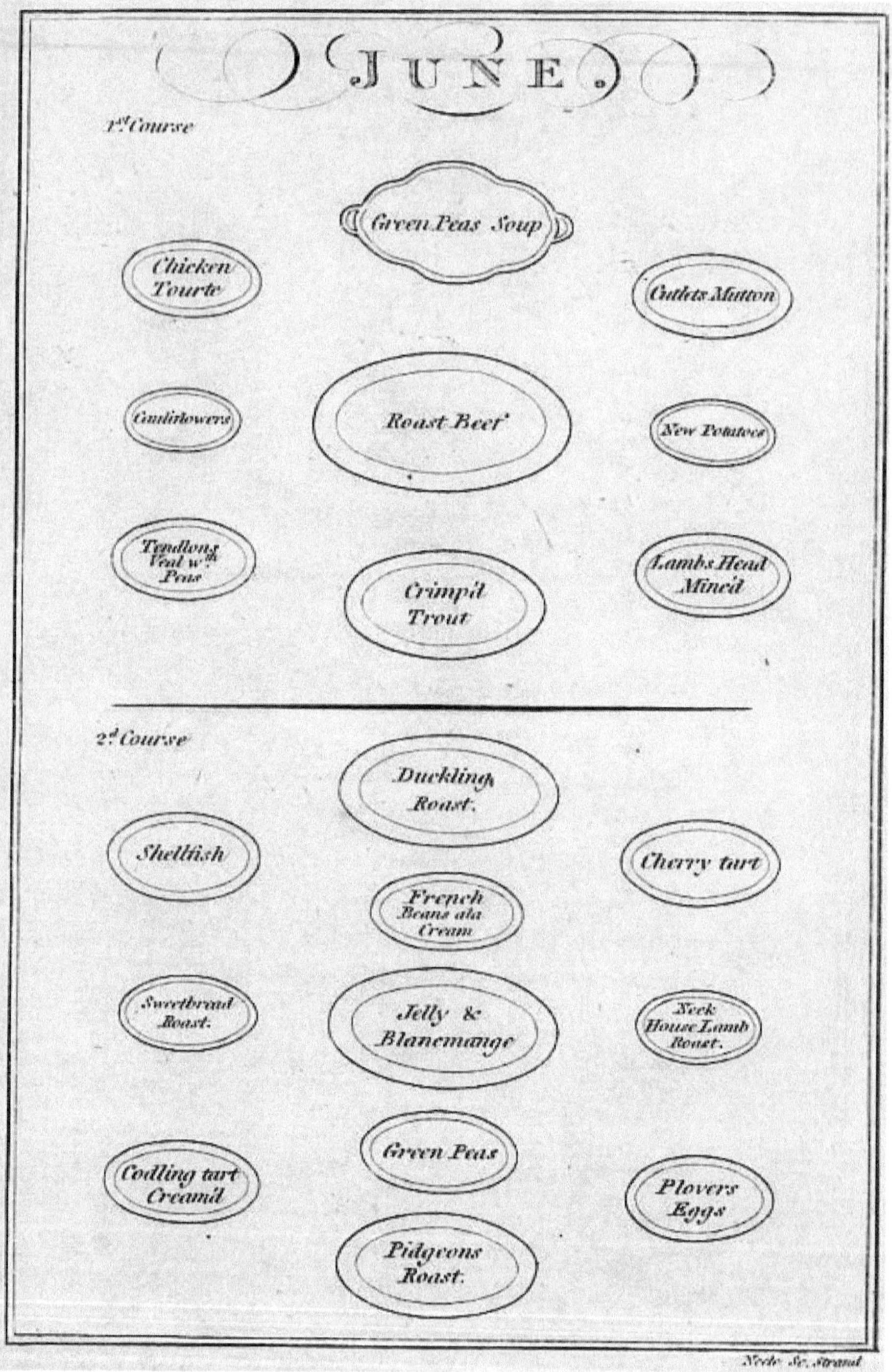

JUNE.

JUNE.

1ˢᵗ· Course

<table>
<tr><td>Chicken
Tourte</td><td>Green Peas Soup</td><td>Cutlets Mutton</td></tr>
<tr><td>Cauliflowers</td><td>Roast Beef</td><td>New Potatoes</td></tr>
<tr><td>Tendlons
Veal wᵗʰ·
Peas</td><td>Crimp'd
Trout</td><td>Lambs Head
Minc'd</td></tr>
</table>

2ᵈ· Course

<table>
<tr><td></td><td>Duckling
Roast.</td><td></td></tr>
<tr><td>Shellfish</td><td></td><td>Cherry Tart</td></tr>
<tr><td></td><td>French Beans ala
Cream</td><td></td></tr>
<tr><td>Sweetbread
Roast.</td><td>Jelly &
Blancmange</td><td>Neck
House Lamb
Roast.</td></tr>
<tr><td></td><td>Green Peas</td><td></td></tr>
<tr><td>Codling tart
Cream'd</td><td></td><td>Plovers
Eggs</td></tr>
<tr><td></td><td>Pidgeons
Roast.</td><td></td></tr>
</table>

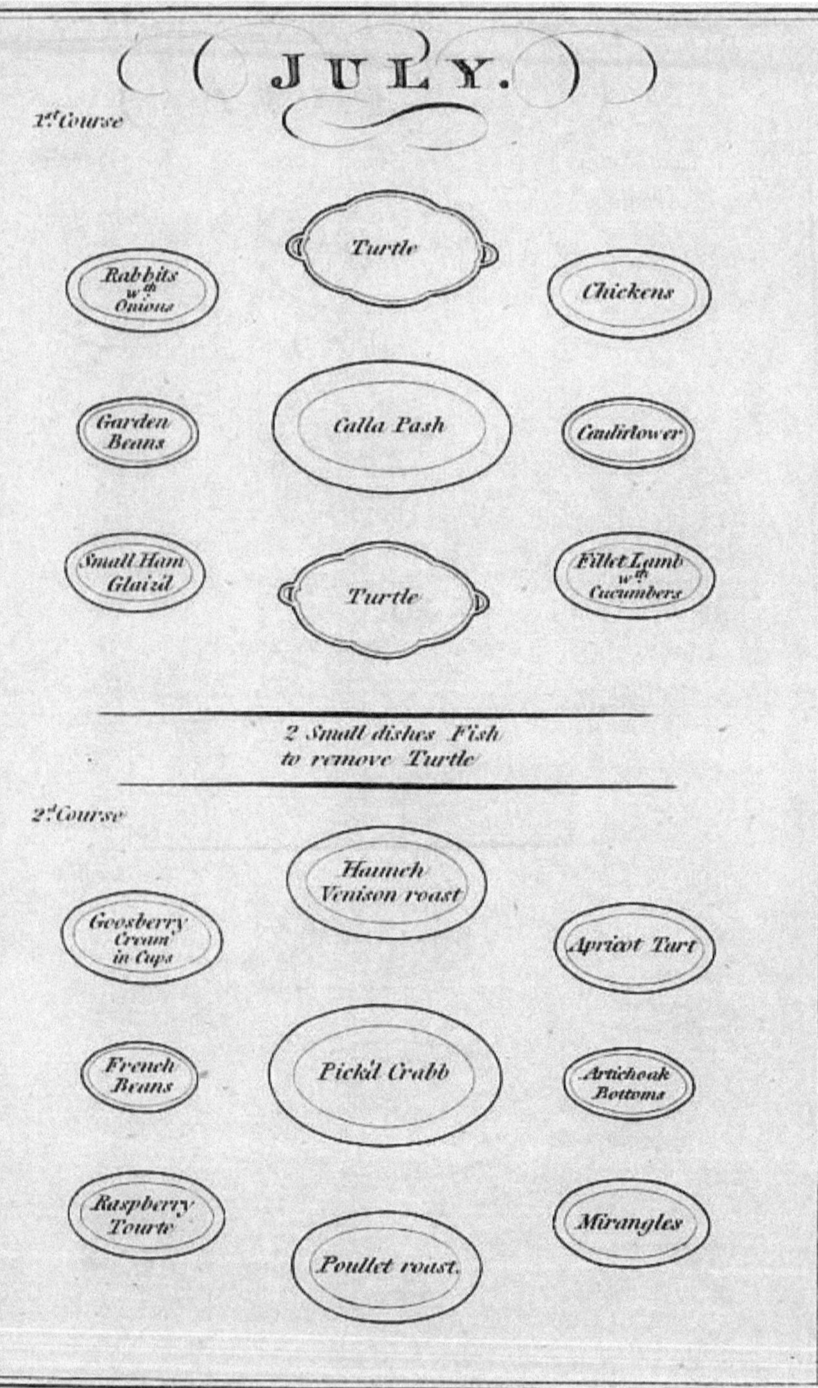

JULY.
1st Course
Turtle
Rabbits wth Onions
Chickens
Garden Beans
Calla Pash
Cauliflower
Small Ham Glaizd
Turtle
Fillet Lamb wth Cucumbers
2 Small dishes Fish to remove Turtle
2d Course
Haunch Venison roast
Goosberry Cream in Cups
Apricot Tart
French Beans
Pick'd Crabb
Artichoak Bottoms
Raspberry Tourte
Mirangles
Poullet roast.
Neele Sc. Strand

JULY.

1st. Course

<table>
<tr><td>*Rabbits*
w^{th.}
Onions</td><td>*Turtle*</td><td></td></tr>
<tr><td></td><td></td><td>*Chickens*</td></tr>
<tr><td>*Garden*
Beans</td><td>*Calla Pash*</td><td>*Cauliflower*</td></tr>
<tr><td></td><td></td><td>*Fillet Lamb*
w^{th.}</td></tr>
<tr><td>*Small Ham*
Glaiz'd</td><td>*Turtle*</td><td>*Cucumbers*</td></tr>
<tr><td></td><td>*2 Small dishes Fish*
to remove Turtle</td><td></td></tr>
</table>

2d. Course

<table>
<tr><td>*Goosberry*
Cream
in Cups</td><td>*Haunch*
Venison roast</td><td>*Apricot Tart*</td></tr>
<tr><td>*French*
Beans</td><td>*Pick'd Crabb*</td><td>*Artichoak*
Bottoms</td></tr>
<tr><td>*Raspberry*
Tourte</td><td>*Poullet roast.*</td><td>*Mirangles*</td></tr>
</table>

AUGUST.

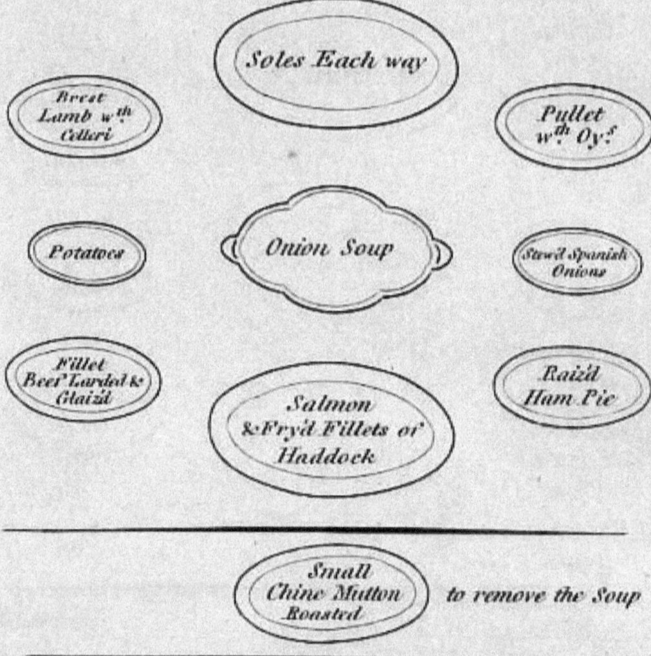

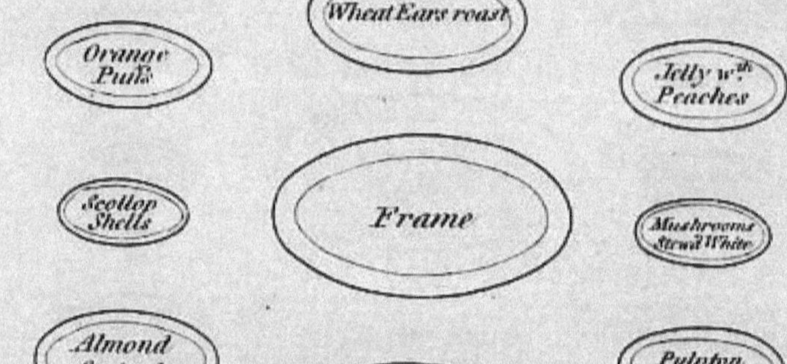

Neele Sc. Strand

AUGUST.

1ˢᵗ· Course

<table>
<tr><td>Brest Lamb
wᵗʰ·
Celleri</td><td>Soles Each way</td><td>Pullet
wᵗʰ· Oyˢ·</td></tr>
<tr><td>Potatoes</td><td>Onion Soup</td><td>Stew'd Spanish
Onions</td></tr>
<tr><td>Fillet
Beef Larded
& Glaiz'd</td><td>Salmon
& Fry'd Fillets of
Haddock</td><td>Raiz'd
Ham Pie</td></tr>
<tr><td></td><td>Small
Chine Mutton
Roasted</td><td>to remove the Soup</td></tr>
</table>

2ᵈ· Course

<table>
<tr><td>Orange
Puffs</td><td>Wheat Ears roast</td><td>Jelly wᵗʰ·
Peaches</td></tr>
<tr><td>Scollop
Shells</td><td>Frame</td><td>Mushrooms
Stew'd White</td></tr>
<tr><td>Almond
Custards</td><td>Levrett
Roast</td><td>Pulpton
of Apples</td></tr>
</table>

SEPTEMBER.

1st Course

a Pike Baked

Fricassee
of
Chickens

Fillet
Mutton & Stew'd
Endive

Fry'd
Celleri

Turnip Soup

French
Sallad

Fillet Pork
Roast

Crimp'd Cod
and
Fry'd Smelts

Cutlets Veal
Larded

2d Course

Partridges
Roast

Ragout of
Sweetbreads

Maccroni

Muffins
push'd dry &
Cherries

Chantillie
Baskett

Damson
Tart

Eggs ala
Trip

Larks Roast

Lambs Fry

SEPTEMBER.

1st. Course

Fricassee   a Pike Baked   Fillet
of   Mutton & Stew'd
Chickens   Endive

Fry'd   French
Celleri   Turnip Soup   Sallad

Fillet Pork   Crimp'd Cod   Cutlets Veal
Roast   and   Larded
                   Fry'd Smelts

2^{d.} Course

                   Partridges
Ragout of   Roast
Sweetbreads   Maceroni

Muffing pud^{s.}   Chantillie   Damson
wth. dry'd   Baskett   Tart
Cherries

Eggs ala   Lambs Fry
Trip
                   Larks Roast

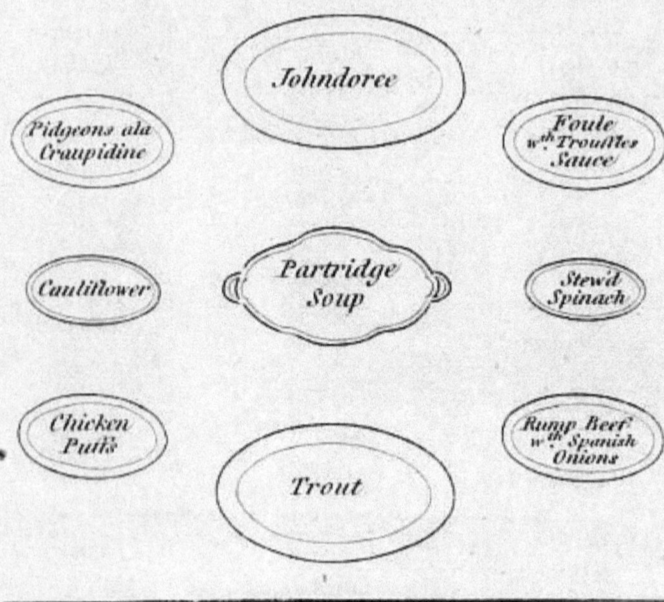

OCTOBER.
1st Course
Johndoree
Pidgeons ala Craupidine
Foule wth Trouffles Sauce
Cauliflower
Partridge Soup
Stew'd Spinach
Chicken Puffs
Rump Beef wth Spanish Onions
Trout

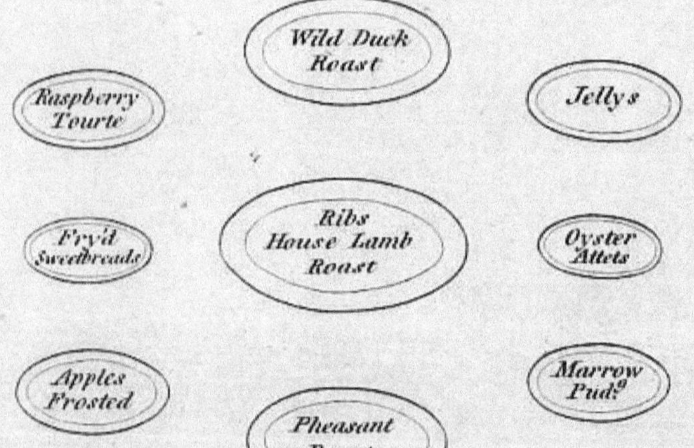

2d Course
Wild Duck Roast
Raspberry Tourte
Jellys
Fry'd Sweetbreads
Ribs House Lamb Roast
Oyster Attets
Apples Frosted
Marrow Pudg
Pheasant Roast

OCTOBER.

1st. Course

Pidgeons ala Craupidine	*Johndoree*	*Foule wth. Trouffles Sauce*
Cauliflower	*Partridge Soup*	*Stew'd Spinach*
Chicken Puffs	*Trout*	*Rump Beef wth. Spanish Onions*

2^{d.} Course

Raspberry Tourte	*Wild Duck Roast*	*Jellys*
Fry'd Sweetbreads	*Ribs House Lamb Roast*	*Oyster Attets*
Apples Frosted	*Pheasant Roast*	*Marrow Pud^{s.}*

NOVEMBER.

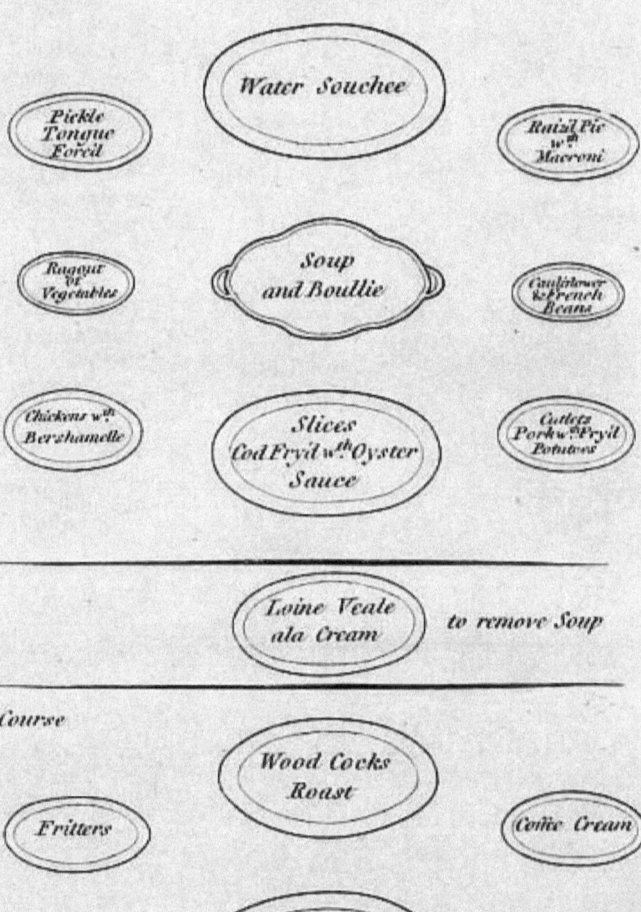

Neele Sc. Strand

NOVEMBER.

1ˢᵗ· Course

Pickle Tongue Forc'd	*Water Souchee*	*Raiz'd Pie wᵗʰ· Macroni*
Ragout of Vegetables	*Soup and Boullie*	*Cauliflower & French Beans*
Chickens wᵗʰ· Bershamelle	*Slices Cod Fry'd wᵗʰ· Oyster Sauce*	*Cutlets Pork wᵗʰ· Fry'd Potatoes*
	Loine Veale ala Cream	*to remove Soup*

2ᵈ· Course

Fritters	*Wood Cocks Roast*	*Coffee Cream*
Jerusalem Artichoaks	*Potted Beef Moddled*	*Stew'd Water Cresses*
Preserved Apricol Tart	*Partridges Roast*	*Golding Pippins wᵗʰ· Jelly*

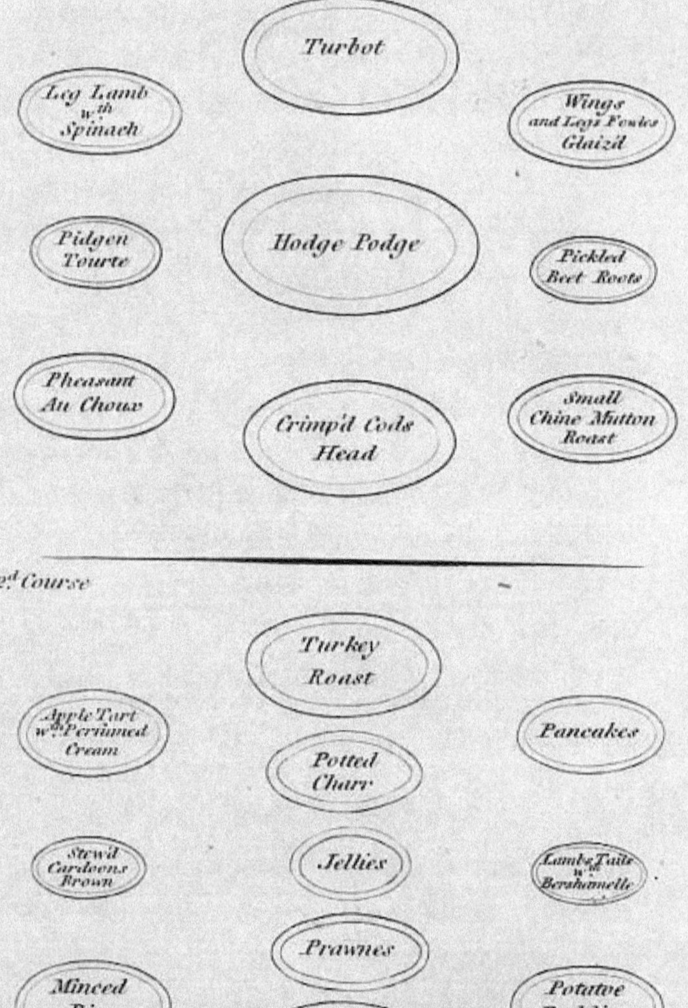
DECEMBER.

1st Course

Turbot

Leg Lamb
wth
Spinach

Wings
and Legs Fowles
Glaiz'd

Pidgen
Tourte

Hodge Podge

Pickled
Beet Roots

Pheasant
Au Choux

Crimp'd Cods
Head

Small
Chine Mutton
Roast

2d Course

Turkey
Roast

Apple Tart
wth Perfumed
Cream

Pancakes

Potted
Charr

Stew'd
Cardoons
Brown

Jellies

Lambs Tails
wth
Berahamelle

Prawnes

Minced
Pies

Potatoe
Pudding

Snipes
Roast

Neele Sc. Strand

DECEMBER.

1ˢᵗ· Course

Leg Lamb *wᵗʰ·* *Spinach*	*Turbot*	*Wings* *and Legs Fowles* *Glaiz'd*
Pidgeon *Tourte*	*Hodge Podge*	*Pickled* *Beet Roots*
Pheasant *Au Choux*	*Crimp'd Cods* *Head*	*Small* *Chine Mutton* *Roast*

2ᵈ· Course

	Turkey *Roast*	
Apple Tart *wᵗʰ· Perfumed* *Cream*		*Pancakes*
	Potted *Charr*	
Stew'd *Cardoons* *Brown*	*Jellies*	*Lambs Tails* *wᵗʰ·* *Bershamelle*
	Prawnes	
Minced *Pies*		*Potatoe Pudding*
	Snipes Roast	

THE ART OF COOKERY

Beef Stock.

CUT chuck beef into pieces, put it into a pot, set it on the fire, with a sufficient quantity of water to cover it. When it boils skim it clean; add a bunch of parsley and thyme, cleaned carrots, leeks, onions, turnips, celery, and a little salt. Let the meat boil till tender, skim off the fat, then strain it through a fine hair sieve.

Veal Stock, for Soups.

TAKE a leg of veal and some lean ham, cut them into pieces, put them into a pan with a quart of water, some peeled carrots, turnips, onions, leeks, and celery; draw them down till nearly tender, but of no colour; then add a sufficient quantity of beef stock to cover the ingredients, boil all together one hour, skim it free from fat, and strain it. Some game drawn down with it will make it excellent.

N. B. I have directed the veal stock not to be drawn down to a colour, as in that state it will answer two purposes; first, for white soups; and, secondly, as it might be coloured with a bright liquid to any height, which will be directed for gravy soups. It frequently happens, likewise, that, if not strictly attended to, it will burn.

Consumé, or the Essence of Meat.

REDUCE veal stock to a good consistence, but be careful not to let it colour.

Cullis, or a thick Gravy.

TAKE slices of ham, veal, celery, carrots, turnips, onions, leeks, a small bunch of sweet herbs, some allspice, black pepper, mace, a piece of lemon-peel, and two bay leaves; put them into a pan with a quart of water, and draw them down till of a light brown colour, but be careful not to let it burn; then discharge it with beef stock. When it boils, skim it very clean from fat, and thicken it with flour and water, or flour and butter passed. Let it boil gently three quarters of an hour; season it to the palate with cayenne pepper, lemon juice, and salt; strain it through a tamis cloth or sieve, and add a little liquid of colour, which may be made as in the following receipt.

Liquid of Colour for Sauces, &c.

PUT a quarter of a pound of the best brown sugar into a frying pan very clean from grease, and half a gill of water; set it over a gentle fire, stirring it with a wooden spoon till it is thoroughly burnt and of a good bright colour, then discharge it with water; when it boils skim it and strain it. Put it by for use in a vessel close covered.

Benshamelle.

TAKE white veal, lean ham, turnips, celery, onions cut in pieces, a blade of mace, a little whole white pepper; sweat them down till three parts tender, then discharge it with beef stock. Let it boil, skim it clean, and thicken with flour and water, or flour and butter passed; add to it a sufficient quantity of cream to make it quite white. Let it simmer gently half an hour, and strain it through a tamis cloth.

N. B. Let it be of the thickness of light batter.

To make a passing of Flour and Butter for Cullis or Benshamelle.

PUT fresh butter into a stewpan over a fire, when it is melted add a sufficient quantity of sifted flour to make it into a paste, and mix them together with a whisk over a very slow fire for ten minutes.

Soup a la Reine.

TAKE three quarts of veal stock with a blade of mace boiled in it; then strain it to the crumb of four penny french rolls, three quarters of a pound of sweet almonds blanched and pounded very fine, likewise the white meat of dressed fowl pounded. Let all simmer together for ten minutes, and rub them through a tamis cloth till the soup is of a proper thickness; season it to the palate with salt; make it boil, and serve it up with a gill of cream in it.

Crayfish Soup.

TAKE three quarts of veal stock, the crumb of four penny french rolls, the meats of a hen lobster, and half a hundred crayfish pounded, with some live lobster spawn; add all together, make it boil, skim it clean, rub it through a tamis cloth, make it of a middling thickness, and season to the palate with salt and a little cayenne pepper. Serve it up with crust of french bread cut into small round pieces.

Vermicelli Soup, white.

TAKE three quarts of veal stock and two ounces of vermicelli, boil them together a quarter of an hour, rub it through a tamis cloth, season with salt, make it boil, skim it, and add a leason. Let it simmer for five minutes.

To make the Leason.

TAKE the yolks of four eggs, half a pint of cream, and a little salt, mixed well together.

Cleared brown Stock for Gravy Soups.

Take three quarts of veal stock perfectly free from fat; add a small quantity of liquid colour to make it of a fine brown; season to the palate with salt and a little cayenne pepper; beat up together two yolks, two whites, and two shells of eggs; whisk them with the stock, set it over a fire, let it boil gently ten minutes, then strain it through a tamis cloth. This stock is required for rice, brown vermicelli, celery, santé, or turnip soups.

N. B. I have directed the brown stock, for gravy soups only, to be cleared with eggs, as that method has been most approved, it being pleasant to the eye, and equally agreeable to the palate.

Rice Soup.

Add to three quarts of cleared stock two ounces of rice, washed, picked, parboiled, and drained dry. Let it boil gently till the rice is tender.

Celery Soup.

Cut celery heads two inches long then, some of the white part into small pieces; wash, blanch, and drain it, and put to it three quarts of cleared stock. Make it boil, skim it, and let the celery simmer till tender.

Turnip Soup.

Pare good and firm turnips, cut them with a knife or scoop into shapes, fry them with a bit of lard till of a light brown colour, then drain and wipe them free from fat (or they may be steamed with a very little water, to prevent them from burning, till they are half done); then put to them cleared stock, and boil them gently till tender.

Cressey Soup.

Take twelve large red carrots, scrape them clean, cut off only the red part in thin slices, and put them in a stewpan with a quart of water; add cleaned turnips, celery, leeks, and onions, cut in pieces, and half a pint of split peas. Stew all together till tender, adding some stock to prevent burning; then rub it through a tamis, and put to the pulp five pints of veal stock and some blanched water-cresses; make it boil for twenty minutes, skim it, season it with salt, and serve it up.

N. B. To be the thickness of peas soup.

Santé, or Spring Soup.

Pare, and cut into shapes, turnips and carrots, likewise celery heads about two inches long; wash them, and steam them separately with a very little water till they are three parts done; then cut the white part of the celery into small pieces, likewise leeks, cabbage, cos lettuces, endive, and chervil, of each a small quantity; blanch and drain them dry, then put all the vegetables together; add to them three quarts of cleared brown stock, and boil them gently till tender. In spring add young green peas, tops of asparagus, and button onions, steamed as the above.

N. B. A small piece of bouillic beef may be stewed till tender; and ten minutes before it is to be served up wipe it dry, and put it into the soup with the vegetables.

Onion Soup.

TAKE eight middling-sized peeled onions, cut them into very thin slices, pass them with a quarter of a pound of fresh butter and flour till tender; then add three quarts of veal stock; make it boil twenty minutes; skim it, season it with salt, and add a leason; mix it well with a whisk, make it simmer, and serve it up.

Green Peas Soup.

TAKE one quart of young green peas, four turnips pared and cut in the form of dice, two cos lettuces cut in small slices, two middling-sized onions cut very fine; wash them, add a quarter of a pound of fresh butter, and stew them till nearly done. Then take two quarts of large fresh green peas, and boil them in three quarts of veal stock till tender; strain and pound them, preserving the liquor; then rub the peas through a tamis, and add the pulp with the liquor to the above herbs, a little flour and water, pepper and salt, and season to the palate, with a bit of sugar if approved. Boil all together half an hour; skim it and when it is to be served up, add the pulp of some boiled parsley rubbed through a tamis to make it look green.

N. B. Cut pieces of bread into thin sippets, dry them before the fire, and serve up on a plate.

Old Peas Soup.

TAKE chuck beef cut into pieces, knuckles of ham and veal, pickle pork cut into square pieces of half a pound each; put all into a pot with peeled turnips, leeks, onions, carrots, and celery, cut into slices, and some old split peas, with a sufficient quantity of water; when it boils, skim it, and add a very small bunch of dried mint. Let the ingredients boil till tender, then take the mint out, rub the soup through a tamis till of a good thickness; when done, add to the liquor, turnips cut in form of dice, celery and leeks cut small and washed. Make the soup boil, skim it, season with pepper and salt, and serve it up with the pork in it. Some bread cut in form of dice, and fried, to be served up on a dish.

N. B. The pork to be taken out when nearly done, and added to the soup half an hour before it is served up.

Peas Soup another way.

PUT the peas with the above-mentioned vegetables into a pot with some water; stew them gently till tender, then add a little dried mint, and rub them through a tamis cloth; put the pulp to some good veal stock, likewise add some turnips pared and cut into forms like dice, some leeks and celery cut small and blanched; season to the palate with pepper and salt; then making it boil, skim it, and stew the herbs till tender. Serve it up with pieces of pickle pork in it.

N. B. The pickle pork to be cut into small square pieces and boiled till nearly done, and then added to the soup a quarter of an hour before it is to be served up to table. Let the soup be of a proper thickness.

Giblet Soup.

LET the giblets be scalded, picked clean, and cut in pieces; which done, put them in a stewpan, season them with herbs and spice, the same as for real turtle; add some veal stock, stew them till nearly done, pick them free from the herbs, chop the bones down, strain, thicken, and season the liquor, as for real turtle; make it boil, then add it to the giblets, stew them till tender, and serve them up with egg and forcemeat balls.

Fish Meagré Soup.

TAKE pieces of different sorts of fish, such as salmon, skate, soles, &c. Sweat them till tender, with turnip, onion, celery, a clove of garlick, and a blade of mace; then add some plain veal broth. Let all simmer together for half an hour; then strain and skim it free from fat; season with salt and cayenne pepper; clear it with white of eggs, and colour with a little saffron.

N. B. It may be served up with celery or rice in it.

Mock Turtle of Calf's Head.

TAKE a scalp cleaned by the butcher, scald it for twenty minutes, then wash it clean, cut it into pieces two inches square, add a gallon of veal stock, and boil them till nearly done. Have ready some pieces of veal cut in form of dice, but four times larger, seasoned with herbs, spices, and onions, the same as real turtle; and strain to it the liquor the scalp is boiled in. Let the meat simmer till almost done; pick it, and add to it the scalp with forcemeat and egg balls; then thicken the liquor as for real turtle, and when it boils skim it clean, put it to the meats, and simmer all together half an hour.

Mutton Broth.

TAKE a neck of mutton cut into pieces, preserving a handsome *piece* to be served up in the tureen. Put all in a stewpot with three quarts of cold beef stock, or water with a little oatmeal mixed in it, some turnips, onions, leeks, celery cut in pieces, and a small bunch of thyme and parsley. When it boils skim it clean, and take the *piece* of mutton out when nearly done, and let the other boil till tender; then have ready turnips cut in form of dice, some leeks, celery, half a cabbage, and parsley, all cut small, and some marigolds; wash them, strain the liquor of the meat, skim it free from fat, add it to the ingredients, with the *piece* of mutton, and a little pearl barley if approved; season with salt, simmer all together till done, and serve it up with toasted bread on a plate.

Real Turtle.

HANG the turtle up by the hind fins, and cut off the head overnight; in the morning cut off the fore fins at the joints, and the callipee all round; then take out the entrails, and be careful not to break the gall; after which cut off the hind fins and all the meat from the bones, callipee and callipash; then chop the callipee and callipash into pieces; scald them together, the fins being whole, but take care not to let the scales set. When cleaned, chop the fins into pieces four inches long; wash the pieces of the callipee, callipash, and fins, and put them into a pot with the bones and a sufficient quantity of water to cover; then add a bunch of sweet herbs and whole onions, and skim it when the liquor boils. When the fins are nearly done take them out, together with the remainder of the turtle, when done, picked free from bone. Then strain the liquor and boil it down till reduced to one third part; after which cut the meat into pieces four times larger than dice; put it into a pot, add a mixture of herbs chopped fine, such as knotted marjoram, savory, thyme, parsley, a very little basil, some chopped onions, some beaten spices, as allspice, a few cloves, a little mace, black pepper, salt, some veal stock, and the liquor that was reduced. Boil the meat till three parts done, pick it free from herbs, strain the liquor through a tamis sieve, make a passing of flour and three quarters of a pound of fresh butter, mixing it well over a fire for some time, and then add to it madeira wine, (if a turtle of seventy pounds weight, three pints,) and the liquor of the meat. When it boils, skim it clean, season to the palate with cayenne pepper, lemon juice, and salt, and strain it to the pieces of fins and shell in one pot, and the lean meat into another; and if the turtle produce any real green fat, let it be boiled till done, then strained, cut into pieces, and added to the fins and shell, and then simmer each meat till tender. When it is to be served up, put a little fat at the bottom of the tureens, some lean in the center, and more fat at the top, with egg and force-meat balls, and a few entrails.

N. B. The entrails must be cleaned well, then boiled in water till very tender, and preserved as white as possible, and just before they are strained off add the balls. If a callipash is served up, the shell to be cut down on each side, and chop the pieces for the soup; the remaining part of the back shell to be pasted round with a raised crust, egged, ornamented, and baked, and the soup served in it in the same manner as in the tureens.

Callipee.

Take a quarter of the under part of a turtle of sixty pounds weight, and scald it, and when done, take the shoulder-bone out and fill the cavity with a good high-seasoned forcemeat made with the lean of the turtle; put it into a stewpan, and add a pint of madeira wine, cayenne pepper, salt, lemon juice, a clove of garlick, a little mace, a few cloves and allspice tied in a bag, a bunch of sweet herbs, some whole onions, and three quarts of good beef stock. Stew gently till three parts done; then take the turtle and put it into another stewpan, with some of the entrails boiled and some egg balls; add a little thickening of flour and butter to the liquor, let it boil, and strain it to the turtle, &c. then stew it till tender, and the liquor almost reduced to a glaize. Serve it up in a deep dish, pasted round as a callipash, ornamented and baked.

N. B. I think the above mode of serving it up in a dish the best, as it frequently happens that the shell of the callipee is not properly baked.

Glaize for Hams, Larding, roasted Poultry, &c.

TAKE a leg of veal, lean of ham, beef, some indifferent fowls, celery, turnips, carrots, onions, leeks cleaned and cut into pieces, a little lemon peel, mace, and black pepper, a small quantity of each; add three quarts of water, sweat them down till three parts done, discharge with water, and boil it till the goodness is extracted; then skim it, and strain the liquor into a large pan. Next day take the fat from it very clean; set the stock over a fire, and when warm clear it with whites and a few yolks of eggs; then add a little colour and strain it through a tamis; boil it quick till reduced to a glaize, and be careful not to let it burn.

N. B. In the same manner may be made glaize of separate herbs or roots, which will be serviceable on board a ship, or in the country, where herbs or roots cannot be procured at all times; and they are to be preserved in bottles, as they will not, when cold, be of a portable substance.

Fish plain boiled to be prepared thus:

PUT them in clean boiling pump water well salted, and when served up to be garnished with fresh picked parsley and scraped horseradish; except salt fish, which should be properly soaked, then cut in pieces and put in cold water, and when it boils let it simmer six or eight minutes, and serve it up on a napkin with boiled parsnips and potatoes round, or on a plate, and egg sauce in a boat.

N. B. Fish should be chosen very fresh and of good appearance, it adding as much to their beauty as gratifying to the palate when dressed, there being in my opinion but two sorts—good and bad. But as an exception to the above observation, skate will be better for eating if kept for one or two days in a cool place before it is dressed.

Fish generally fried.

PIECES of skate.
Whitings.
Fillets of haddocks.
Smelts.
Soles.
Perch.
Flounders.
Slices of hollibut.
Slices of cod.

To prepare the above for frying, &c.

WIPE the different sorts of fish dry, beat yolk of eggs, and spread it over them with a paste brush; then put crumbs of bread over the egg. Have plenty of lard in an iron frying pan, and when it almost boils put a proper quantity and fry them of a fine gold colour; drain them dry, and serve them up with fried parsley.

N. B. The crumbs to be rubbed through a hair sieve. The parsley also to be picked, washed, and dried with a cloth, then to be put into the lard not very hot, and fried of a green colour. Sprinkle a little salt over.

Broiled Fish prepared thus:

WIPE the fish dry, flour them well, and have the gridiron clean; then rub the bars with a veal caul, and put the fish at a proper distance. Broil them gently over a clear coal fire till of a fine colour, and serve them up directly.

N. B. Fish in general to be floured, except herrings, which are only to be scored with a knife, and the following methods of broiling other fish to be observed.

Broiled Salmon to be prepared thus:

TAKE pieces or slices of salmon, wipe them dry, dip them in sweet oil, and season with pepper and salt; fold them in pieces of writing paper, broil over a clear fire, and serve them up very hot.

N. B. In the same manner are to be done red mullets, &c.

Broiled Mackarel, common way.

WIPE them dry, split them down the back, sprinkle with pepper and salt, and broil them gently.

To stew Fish.

ADD to some cullis a few chopped eshallots, anchovies, a bay leaf, horseradish scraped, a little quantity of lemon peel, and some red port; season it well with cayenne pepper, salt, and juice of lemon, and when it boils let it be of a proper thickness, and strain it to the fish; then stew it gently, and serve it up in a deep dish with the liquor, and fried bread round it. If carp or tench, some of the hard roe mixed in batter and fried in pieces. The roes likewise of different fish may be stewed in the same manner, and served up as a dish of themselves. Eels, soles, or other fish may be done the same way.

Water souchée of Perch, Flounders, Soles, Eels, &c.

TAKE perch cleaned and fresh crimped; put them into boiling pump water well-seasoned with salt, and when they boil, skim them clean. Take them out with a large skimmer, put them into a deep dish, strew parsley roots and scalded parsley over, and add some of the liquor. Serve them up as hot as possible, with slices of brown bread and butter on a plate.

N. B. The time the fish are to boil must be according to their size; and the parsley roots are to be cleaned, cut into slips, and boiled by themselves till tender.

Roasted Pike or Sturgeon.

LET the fish be well cleaned, then make a stuffing of capers, anchovies, parsley and thyme chopped fine, a little grated nutmeg and lemon peel, pepper, salt, breadcrumbs, fresh butter, and an egg. Fill the fish and sew it up; turn it round, and fasten the head with the tail; then egg the fish over and breadcrumb it; after which bake or roast it gently till done, and of a good brown colour. Serve it up with a sauce over, made of cullis, fresh butter, cayenne, anchovie essence, and lemon pickle.

Bacquillio with Herbs.

LET the fish be well soaked; then boil them and pick free from bone. Wash and chop small some spinach, sorrel, green onions, and parsley; after which add fresh butter, essence of anchovies, cayenne pepper, and plenty of the juice of seville oranges. Sweat the herbs down, add the fish, and simmer them till tender.

Entrée of Eels.

TAKE good-sized eels, bone and cut them in pieces of three inches long; pass them over a slow fire in a small quantity of sweet herbs and eshallots, fresh butter, pepper, salt, and lemon juice. When three parts done put all on a dish, dip each piece in the liquor, breadcrumb, and broil them over a clear fire. Serve them up with anchovie sauce in a boat.

Entrée of Soles.

LET good-sized soles be cleaned and filletted; roll them up, put them into a stewpan, add a little fresh butter, lemon juice, pepper, and salt, and simmer them over a slow fire till done. Serve them up with a sauce over, made of button onions, mushrooms, egg balls, pickle cucumbers scooped round, slices of sweetbreads, and good strong cullis coloured with lobster spawn.

N. B. The above fillets may be fried, and served up with the sauce round.

Entrée of Whitings, &c.

TAKE fillets of haddocks or whitings, wet them with whites of eggs, and lay upon them slices of salmon, seasoned with pepper and salt. Put them into a stewpan with a little fresh butter; stew the fish over a slow fire till done, with the pan close covered. Serve them up with a sauce over, made with chopped parsley, chopped mushrooms and eshallots, a little rhenish wine, mustard, and cullis, mixed and boiled together for ten minutes.

Entrée of Salmon.

MAKE white paper cases, and put a little sweet oil at the bottom of each. Cut into pieces some fresh salmon, pepper and salt them, and put them into the cases; then set them over a fire on a baking plate and in a stewpan covered over, with a fire at top and bottom. When broiled enough, serve them up with poached eggs on the top of the salmon, and anchovie sauce in a boat.

Entrée of Smelts, &c.

CLEAN, turn round, and fry of a good colour, some fresh smelts; then three parts boil a slice of fresh crimped cod cut two inches thick; pull it into flakes, have ready some benshamelle, whisk it with the yolks of two eggs, add the flakes of the cod, season with salt and lemon juice to the palate, and simmer the fish over a slow stove till done. Serve it up with the fried smelts round the dish, and a few over the stew.

Entrée of Mackarel.

SPLIT them down the back, season with pepper and salt, and lay a sprig of fennel in them. Broil them gently, and when served up, the fennel to be taken out, and a mixture of fresh butter, chopped parsley, green onions, pepper, salt, and plenty of lemon juice to be put in its stead.

Mackarel the German way.

SPLIT them down the back and season with pepper and salt; broil them, and serve them up with the following sauce in a boat:—pick and wash fennel, parsley, mint, thyme, and green onions, a small quantity of each. Boil them tender in a little veal broth; then chop and add to them some fresh butter, the liquor, a grated nutmeg, the juice of half a lemon, a little cayenne pepper and salt. Let it boil, and make it of a proper thickness with flour and water.

Olios, or a Spanish Dish.

THE articles that are wanted consist of the following: viz.

    Leg of mutton of ten pounds.
    Leg of veal ditto.
    Chuck beef ditto.
    Lean ham six pounds.
    Best end of a neck of mutton.
    Breast of veal, small.
    Two pieces of bouillie beef of one pound each.
    Two pair of pigs feet and ears.
    A bologna sausage.
    A fowl.
    A pheasant.
    Two partridges.
    Two ruffs and rees.
    Two quails.
    Two teal.
    Two pigeons.
    Two rabbits.
    One hare.
    Two stags tongues.
    One quart of burgonza peas.
    Turnips.

Carrots.
Celery.
Onions.
Leeks.
Parsley.
Thyme.
Garlick.
Allspice.
Cloves.
Mace.
Nutmegs.
Black pepper.
Haricot roots.
Fried bread.
Eggs.
Saffron, and
Lemons.

The Olio to be made as follows:

TAKE the beef, veal, mutton, and ham; cut them into pieces, put them into a pot, cover with water, and when it boils skim clean; then add carrots, celery, turnips, onions, leeks, garlick, parsley, and thyme, tied in a bunch; allspice, cloves, nutmeg, black pepper, mace, and a little ginger, put in a cloth. Boil all together till it becomes a strong stock, and strain it. Then cut the breast of veal into tendrons, and best end of neck of mutton into steaks, and half fry them; pigs feet and ears cleaned; hare cut into joints and daubed with bacon; bouillie beef tied round with packthread; poultry trussed very neat, with the legs drawn in close; the tongues scalded and cleaned; and the rabbits cut into pieces. When the different articles are ready, blanch and wash them, then braise each in a separate stewpan, with the stock that was strained. When the different things are braised enough, pour the liquors from them into a pan, leaving a little with each to preserve from burning. When they are to be served up, skim the liquor very clean, and clear it with whites of eggs; then cut turnips and carrots into haricots, some button onions peeled, and heads of celery trimmed neat; after which blanch them, cut the bologna sausage into slices, boil the burgonza peas till three parts done, then mix all together, add some of the cleared liquor, and stew them gently till done. The remainder of the liquor to be coloured with a little saffron, and served up in a tureen with a few burgonza peas in it.

When the olio is to be served up, take a very large deep dish, make several partitions in it with slips of fried bread dipped in whites of eggs, and set it in a slow oven or before a fire; then lay the tendrons, birds, beef, mutton, fowls, &c. alternately in the partitions, and serve up with the haricot roots, &c. over.

N. B. The whole of the liquor to be seasoned to the palate with cayenne pepper and lemon juice.

[This receipt for a Spanish olio is only written to shew how expensive a dish may be made, and which I saw done. As a substitute I have introduced the following english one, which has been generally approved; and I think, with particular attention, it will exceed the former in flavour.]

Hodge Podge, or English Olio.

Take four beef tails cut into joints, bouille beef two pieces about a quarter of a pound each, and two pieces of pickle pork of the same weight. Put them into a pot, cover with water, and when it boils skim clean, and add half a savoy, two ounces of champignons, some turnips, carrots, onions, leeks, celery, one bay leaf, whole black pepper, a few allspice, and a small quantity of mace. When the meats are nearly done, add two quarts of strong veal stock, and when tender take them out, put them into a deep dish, and preserve them hot till they are to be served up; then strain the liquor, skim it free from fat, season to the palate with cayenne pepper, a little salt, and lemon juice, and add a small quantity of colour; then have ready turnips and carrots cut into haricots, some celery heads trimmed three inches long, and some whole onions peeled. Let them be sweated down, till three parts tender, in separate stewpans, and strain the essences of them to the above liquor; clear it with whites of eggs, strain it through a tamis cloth, mix the vegetables, add the liquor to them, boil them gently for ten minutes, and serve them over the meats.

Light Forcemeat for Pies or Fowls, &c.

Cut in pieces lean veal, ham, and fat bacon; add chopped parsley, thyme, eschallots, a little beaten spices, juice of lemon, pepper and salt, a few cleaned mushrooms, or mushroom powder. Put over a slow fire till three parts done; then pound in a marble mortar till very fine, and add a sufficient quantity of yolk of raw eggs and breadcrumbs to bind it.

Forcemeat Balls for Ragouts, &c.

Cut lean veal and beef suet into small pieces, and add chopped parsley, thyme, marjoram, savory, eschallots, pepper, salt, breadcrumbs, a little grated nutmeg, and yolk of raw eggs. Pound all well together, and roll into balls.

N. B. The balls should be boiled or fried before they are added to any thing.

Egg for Balls.

Boil six eggs, take the yolks, pound them, and add a little flour and salt, and the yolks of two raw eggs. Mix all well together, and roll into balls. They must be boiled before added to any made dish or soup.

Omlets of Eggs for garnishing or cutting in Slips.

Take eggs, break them, and put the yolks and whites into separate pans; beat them up with a little salt, and then put them again into separate earthen vessels rubbed with sweet oil. Have ready a pot of boiling water over a fire, put them in close covered, and let the omlets steam till thoroughly done.

Ox Cheek.

Bone and wash clean the cheek; then tie it up like a rump of beef, put it in a braising pan with some good stock (or water); when it boils, skim it, add two bay leaves, a little garlick, some onions, champignons, celery, carrots, half a small cabbage, turnips, a bundle of sweet herbs, whole black pepper, a little allspice and mace. Let the cheek stew till near done, then cut off the strings, put the cheek in a clean stewpan, strain the liquor through a sieve, skim off the fat very clean, season with lemon juice, cayenne pepper and salt, add a little colour, clear it with eggs, strain it through a tamis cloth to the cheek, and stew it till tender.

Beef Tails.

Cut the tails into joints, and blanch and wash them; then braise them till tender, drain them dry, and serve them up with haricot sauce over.

Haricot Sauce.

Take clean turnips and carrots, and scoop or cut them into shapes, some celery heads cut about two inches long, button onions peeled, some dry or green morells, and artichoke bottoms cut into pieces. Let them all be blanched in separate stewpans till three parts done; then drain and put them all together with some small mushrooms stewed, and a good cullis well-seasoned, and simmer the vegetables till done.

Beef Collops.

Take the fillet from the under part of a rump of beef, cut it into small thin slices, and fry them till three parts done; then add to them slices of pickle cucumbers, small mushrooms stewed, blanched oysters, some good-seasoned cullis, and stew them till tender.

Fillet of Beef larded.

Take a fillet or piece of a rump, force it and lard it with bacon, turn it round like a fillet of veal, roast it, glaize the top, and serve it up with the following sauce made with cullis, lemon pickle, and ketchup; add likewise some scalded celery heads and button onions; then stew till tender, and put the sauce round the beef.

Beef Pallets.

Scald and scale the pallets clean, and boil them till tender; when cool roll them up with forcemeat in the middle, and tie them with thread; braise them as white as possible and serve them up with a sauce made of ham, breast of fowl, pickle cucumbers, omlets of eggs, and good-seasoned cullis or benshamelle.

N. B. The ham, &c. are to be cut in the form of dice, and the omlets made as omlets for garnishing.

Rump of Beef a-la-daube, or braised.

BONE a rump of beef and daub it with slips of fat bacon, seasoned with sweet herbs, eschallots, beaten spices, pepper, and salt. Bind it round with packthread, and braise it till tender; then wipe it dry, glaize the top, and serve it up with the sauce round. Either Spanish onion sauce, or savoy, haricot, or ashée sauce may be used.

N. B. It may be served with the sauce either plain or daubed.

To make Spanish Onion Sauce.

BRAISE six Spanish onions with the beef till three parts done; then peel them, and add some good cullis, seasoned with cayenne pepper, salt, lemon juice, and a little sifted lump sugar, and stew them till tender.

Savoy Sauce.

CUT some savoys in quarters, blanch them, and then tie them round and braise them with the beef till half done. Take them out of the liquor, cut off the string, and put them into a stewpan with good strong cullis, and simmer them till tender.

Ashée Sauce.

TAKE some pickle cucumbers chopped small, then capers, parsley, eschallots, breast of a fowl, lean of ham, carrots, and yolks and whites of eggs. Then add to them a good-seasoned cullis and a little mushroom ketchup. Simmer all together a quarter of an hour.

N. B. The ham, fowl, egg, and carrot to be boiled before they are chopped.

Brisket of Beef with Spanish Onions.

To be done in the same manner as the rump, but not to be daubed with bacon.

Brisket of Beef with Ashée or Haricot.

To be done in the same manner as the preceding.

Rump of Beef a-la mode.

BONE the rump, daub it with slips of fat bacon seasoned with sweet herbs, beaten spices, and pepper and salt. Bind it round with packthread, put it into a braising pan, cover it with some veal stock, make it boil, skim it, and add a pint of red port, some onions, turnips, celery, a few bay leaves, garlick, champignons, a few whole allspice, and a little mace. Let it stew till nearly done; then take it out of the liquor, cut off the strings, wipe it dry, and put it into a clean stewpan. Then strain the liquor, skim the fat off clean, season with cayenne, salt, a gill of vinegar, lemon pickle, and a small quantity of juice of lemon; add a little colour, clear it with whites of eggs, and strain it through a tamis cloth to the beef. Stew it gently till done, and serve it up in a deep dish.

N. B. To the liquor, when cleared with eggs and strained, may be added some passing of flour and butter, by way of thickening, if approved. The reason for clearing the liquor is, that it will make it appear bright either thickened or plain.

Baked Beef.

Bone a leg of beef, wash it clean, chop plenty of parsley, a middling quantity of thyme, eschallots, marjoram, savory, and a little basil. Then mix them together, and add a small quantity of beaten allspice, mace, cloves, pepper, and salt. Rub the beef well with the ingredients, set it in an earthen pan, put to it a gill of vinegar, half a pint of red port, eight middling-sized whole onions peeled, two bay leaves, a few fresh or dried champignons. Let the meat remain till next day; then add a sufficient quantity of water to it, cover the pan close, and bake the meat till tender.

Marrow Bones.

Chop the bones at each end so as to stand steady; then wash them clean, saw them in halves, set them upright in a saucepan with water, and boil them two hours. Serve them up very hot, and with fresh toasted bread.

Mutton Rumps marinated.

Clean and cut the rumps of an equal length, and lay them in a pan and the marinate liquor for a whole night; then pass them in butter till nearly done. Lay them on a dish to cool, wash them over with yolk of egg, and breadcrumb them. Fry them gently in boiling lard till done, and of a nice colour. Drain them dry, and serve them up with a very good-seasoned cullis sauce and ketchup in it.

N. B. In the same manner may be done mutton steaks.

To make Marinate.

Take a little gravy, vinegar, salt, whole black pepper, a few bay leaves, onions sliced, a clove of garlick, and a little thyme. Boil all together and strain it.

Haricot Mutton Cutlets.

Cut a loin or best end of a neck of mutton into steaks, trim them neat, and fry them till three parts done, and of a nice colour. Put them into a stewpan, add a little liquor to preserve them from burning, and simmer till tender. Lay the steaks round in a dish, and serve them up with haricot sauce over.

N. B. The essence that the steaks were stewed in to be strained, skimmed clean from fat, and added to the sauce.

Fillet of Mutton with Cucumbers.

Take the best end of a neck of mutton, cut off the under bone, leaving the long ones on; then trim it neat, lard it, or let it remain plain; roast it gently, glaize it, and serve it up with cucumber sauce under.

Stewed Cucumbers.

Take fresh gathered cucumbers, pare them, cut them into shapes if seedy, or slices if young. Put them into a stewpan, and add a little salt, vinegar, and an onion. Simmer them over a fire till nearly done and the liquor reduced, or fry them with a bit of fresh butter, and add a good strong cullis. Let the cucumbers stew till done, and serve them up with the mutton, which may be roasted with larding (or plain).

N. B. The cucumbers may be served as an entrée of itself, and fried bread put round them.

Mutton Cutlets with Potatoes.

Cut a loin of mutton into steaks, beat them with a chopper, and trim them neat. Pass them in sweet herbs, eschallots, pepper, salt, and lemon juice. When nearly done, lay them on a dish till almost cool, and then egg, breadcrumb, and fry them in boiling lard till of a light brown colour. Place the steaks round in a dish, leaving a cavity in the center, which is to be filled up with potatoes, and the sauce under the steaks.

N. B. The potatoes to be peeled, scooped, or cut into shapes. Then fry them of a light colour, and put them before the fire till wanted; and add to the sauce the steaks were passed in, a little cullis and ketchup; then strain and reduce it almost to a glaize.

Mutton Cutlets a la Maintenon.

Get the best end of a loin of mutton, take off the under bone, and cut it into chops; beat them, and trim them neat; then add to them a bit of fresh butter, chopped parsley, thyme, eschallots, pepper, salt, a little pounded mace, and lemon juice. Pass them till nearly done; then lay them on a dish, pour the liquor over the chops, and, when nearly cool, breadcrumb, and put them separately in oiled white paper; fold them up, broil them over a slow fire, and serve them up with hot poivrade sauce in a boat.

N. B. See *Poivrade Sauce* receipt.

Cutlets a la Irish Stew.

Get the best end of a neck of mutton, take off the under bone, and cut it into chops; season them with pepper, salt, a little mushroom powder, and beaten mace. Put them into a stewpan, add a large onion sliced, some parsley and thyme tied in a bunch, and a pint of veal broth. Simmer the chops till three parts done, then add some whole potatoes peeled, and let them stew till done. Serve it up in a deep dish.

N. B. Let the parsley and thyme be taken out when the stew is to be served up.

Pork Cutlets with Red or White Cabbage.

Take a piece of back pork, cut it into chops, beat and trim them, season with pepper and salt, broil them gently till done and of a light brown colour. Serve them up with stewed red or white cabbage under.

To stew Cabbage.

CUT the cabbage into slips, and blanch and drain them dry. Put them into a stewpan, with a bit of fresh butter, pepper, salt, an onion, some vinegar, half a pint of veal broth, and a little allspice tied in a cloth. Stew the cabbage gently till done and the liquor nearly reduced, and then take the spice and onion out.

Pork Cutlets with Robert Sauce.

GET a piece of back pork, or the best end of a loin, and take off the under bone; then cut the chops neat, season with pepper and salt, broil them gently, and serve them up with the sauce underneath.

To make Robert Sauce.

TAKE some cullis, a bay leaf, an onion sliced, a blade of mace, a little mustard, and a gill of rhenish wine. Boil all together a quarter of an hour, strain it, and reduce it nearly to a glaize.

Pork Cutlets another way.

TRIM the chops neat as above, pass them with a bit of fresh butter, chopped eschallots, pepper, salt, and a little lemon juice. When nearly done, breadcrumb and broil them till of a light brown colour. Serve them up with the following sauce placed underneath; that is to say, cullis, mushroom, ketchup, lemon pickle, and mustard, a little of each, and reduce nearly to a glaize.

Fillet of Pork roasted.

TAKE a piece of back pork, cut the chine bone from the under part, and lay it in a marinate all night. When it is to be roasted run a lark spit through, tie it on another spit, cover it with paper, and roast it gently; and when to be served up, if not coloured enough, glaize it lightly, and put some robert sauce underneath.

Pigs Feet and Ears.

TAKE prepared feet and pass them, with chopped parsley, thyme, eschallots, pepper, salt, and lemon juice. When done, breadcrumb and broil them gently. Let the ears be cut in slices, and add cullis well-seasoned; then stew them for ten minutes, and serve them up with the feet over.

To prepare Pigs Feet and Ears.

SCALD and clean them; then split the feet and tie them round with packthread; put them in a pot covered with water; make it boil, skim it clean, and add a little garlick, thyme, eschallots, onions, bay leaves, whole black pepper, allspice, mace, salt, and udder of veal. Braise them till tender, and put them in an earthen pan for use.

Compotte of Pigeons.

CUT off the pinions, draw the legs in close, colour the breast in boiling hot lard, and then blanch and wash them; which done, put them in a stewpan, add a little veal broth, and simmer them gently till nearly done, and then make a ragout of blanched sweetbreads, button mushrooms, truffles, morells, artichoke bottoms, egg balls, cullis, and the liquor of the pigeons strained, and season well to the palate. Let the ingredients stew for ten minutes, then add them to the pigeons, and serve up all together in a deep dish.

Pigeons a la Craupidine.

CUT off the pinions, draw in the legs, cut the breast so as to lay back, then pass them with sweet herbs, mushrooms, eschallots chopped fine, a little fresh butter, grated nutmeg, lemon juice, pepper, and salt. Let them simmer till nearly done; then lay them on a dish, and when nearly cool, egg with yolk of eggs, and strew them with crumbs of bread rubbed through a fine hair sieve. Fry them of a light colour in boiling hot lard (or broil them). Serve them up with a good cullis and sharp sauce underneath.

Pigeons glaized.

PUT some good-seasoned forcemeat in the pigeons, cut off the pinions, lay back the legs, blanch them, and roast them gently with vine leaves and bards of fat bacon over them. When they are to be served up glaize the top part, and serve them with cullis sauce, or celery heads, or asparagus tops, &c. under them.

Pigeons a la Sousell.

BONE the legs and wings of four pigeons and draw them in; then fill them with a high-seasoned forcemeat, and braise them in a half pint of veal stock. When done enough, take the pigeons out, wipe them dry, glaize the top, and serve them up with stewed sorrel underneath.

N. B. The liquor they were braised in to be strained, skimmed free from fat, and reduced almost to a glaize, and added to the sorrel. (Or they may, when three parts done, be wiped dry, egged and breadcrumbed over, then fried in boiling lard, and served up with sorrel sauce underneath as above).

Hashed Calf's Head.

TAKE a head, without the scalp, chopped in half; wash and blanch it, peel the tongue, cut it in slices, and likewise the meat from the head. Add blanched morells and truffles, egg and forcemeat balls, stewed mushrooms, artichoke bottoms, and well-seasoned cullis. Let the meat stew gently till nearly done, and then add slices of throat sweetbreads. When it is to be served up, put round the hash the brains and rashers of bacon; and, if approved, half the head to be put on the top, which is to be prepared thus:—One half of the head when blanched to be done over with yolk of raw egg; then season with pepper and salt, strew with fine breadcrumbs, bake till very tender, and colour with a salamander if requisite. The brains to be egged and rolled in breadcrumbs, and fried in boiling lard. The rashers of bacon to be broiled.

Breast of Veal en Gallentine.

BONE the veal and lay a light forcemeat over it, and upon that some slips of lean ham, pickle cucumbers, fat bacon, and omlets of eggs white and yellow. Roll it up tight in a cloth, tie each end, and braise it till tender. When it is to be served up, take it out of the cloth, wipe it dry, and glaize the top; then put under it stewed sorrel or stewed celery heads, or ragout.

Breast of Veal Ragout.

TAKE off the under bone and cut the breast in half, lengthways; then cut them in middling-sized pieces, fry them in a little lard till of a light brown colour, wipe them dry, put them into a stewpan with half a pint of veal stock, simmer them till nearly done and the liquor almost reduced; then add blanched morell, truffles, slices of throat sweetbread, egg balls, artichoke bottoms, a little ketchup, and some cullis; season to the palate with cayenne pepper and salt, and a little lemon juice. Let all stew together till done.

Neck of Veal en Erison.

CUT off the scragg and the under chine bone, then lay a light forcemeat on the top of the veal about half the way, and wash it with whites of eggs with a paste brush, and work a sprig or any other device as fancy directs, with pickle cucumber, ham, breast of fowl, omlets of eggs white and yellow, boiled carrots, and some capers. Put the veal into a stewpan, add a little stock, and stew it gently till tender, taking care the ornament is not disturbed. When it is to be served up glaize the plain part, and put under a cullis sauce with asparagus or peas.

N. B. In the same manner may be done heart sweetbreads.

Neck of Veal larded.

TAKE off the under bone of a neck of veal, leave only a part of the long bones on; trim it neat, lard it, and roast it gently with a veal caul over. Ten minutes before it is done take off the caul, and let the veal be of a very light colour. When it is to be served up glaize it, and put under some sorrel sauce, celery heads, or asparagus tops.

Veal Cutlets larded.

CUT the best end of a neck of veal into chops, leaving only a part of the long bone; then lard, blanch, and braise them; and when they are to be served up, drain, dry, glaize, and place them round each other in a dish, and put green truffle sauce, or white mushroom sauce, in the center.

Loin of Veal a la Cream.

TAKE the best end of a loin of veal, joint it, and cut a little of the suet from the kidney; cause it to lay flat, and then make an incision in the center of the top part about three inches deep and six inches long. Take the piece out, chop it, add to it the suet or beef marrow, parsley, thyme, green truffles, mushrooms, eschallots, lemon peel, chopped very fine, and season it with pepper and salt, and a little beaten spice. Put all together into a marble mortar, add the yolks of two eggs, and a little french bread soaked in cream; then pound the ingredients well, and fill the cavity with the forcemeat, and cover it with a piece of veal caul; after which tie it down close and cover the whole with a large piece of caul, roast it gently, and when it is to be served up, take off the large piece of caul, let it colour a little, glaize it lightly, and put under it a benshamelle or a ragout of sweetbreads, &c.

N. B. In the same manner may be done a fillet of veal instead of plain stuffing.

Veal Tendrons (brown or white).

TAKE a breast of white veal, cut off the under bone and the top skin; then cut it into three long slips, and the slips again into pieces of two inches thick; blanch and put them into a stewpan, then add a little water, bards of bacon, and slices of lemon. Braise them till tender, drain them dry, and serve them up with green truffle sauce, or celery, asparagus, or peas. The sauce to be served over the veal.

Celery Sauce, (white), for Veal, Chickens, Turkies, &c.

CUT celery heads three inches long, trim them, wash and blanch them, drain them dry, add a little stock, boil them till nearly done, and the liquor almost reduced; then put to them some benshamelle, and, if approved, five minutes before the sauce is put over the meat or poultry, add a leason of two yolks of eggs and cream.

Celery Sauce, (brown,) for Pullets, &c.

DRESS celery heads as above, but instead of benshamelle add a good cullis only.

N. B. The above sauces may be served up in dishes with fried bread round the celery heads, as an entrée of itself.

Veal Cutlets au natural.

CUT the best end of a neck of veal into chops, trim off the bone, pass the steaks with a bit of fresh butter, chopped parsley, thyme, and eschallots, and season with pepper, salt, and lemon juice. When nearly done, lay them on a dish with the liquor; and when cool, egg, breadcrumb, and broil them gently. Serve them up placed round each other, with a sauce in the center made with cullis, a little ketchup, lemon pickle, and artichoke bottoms cut into pieces.

Veal Collops (brown).

Cut veal cutlets (taken from the fillet) into small thin pieces, and fry them in a little boiling lard till of a light brown colour. Drain them dry, put them into a stewpan, add cullis, stewed mushrooms, some blanched truffles, morells, pieces of artichoke bottoms, some slices of throat sweetbreads, and egg balls. Let them simmer over a slow fire till tender, season to the palate, and serve them up with rashers of broiled bacon round them.

Veal Collops (white).

Cut the collops as for brown, but instead of frying, put them into a stewpan with a bit of fresh butter, a little lemon juice, and a blade of mace. Simmer them till nearly done, then strain the liquor to some benshamelle, and add the collops with some slices of throat sweetbreads, some cocks combs blanched, egg balls, pieces of artichoke bottoms, and stewed white mushrooms. Let them stew gently, season to the palate with salt, and make the sauce of a sufficient thickness to adhere to the ingredients.

N. B. Five minutes before the collops are to be served up a leason may be added of eggs and cream.

Fricando Veal.

Cut off a long or round piece of veal from the leg, beat it flat with a chopper, and make an incision in the under part. Put into it a little light forcemeat, sew it up, lard the top part with pieces of fat bacon very neat, blanch it, put it into a stewpan with a little stock, and cover it close; then let it stew till very tender, and the liquor nearly reduced. When it is to be served up glaize the larding, and put stewed sorrel under.

N. B. The forcemeat, if not approved, may be omitted; and instead of only one piece of veal, three or four small pieces may be served on a dish.

Sorrel Sauce.

Wash clean, squeeze and chop fine, plenty of sorrel, and put it into a stewpan with a bit of fresh butter; stew it till the liquor is almost reduced, and then add a little strong cullis. Let the sauce be of a good thickness.

Veal Olives.

Cut thin bards of fat bacon of six inches long and four broad, lay upon them very thin slices of veal of the same dimensions, wash the veal with yolk of egg, and put upon it some light forcemeat. Then roll them up, run a lark spit through sideway of each olive, tie a string over them to prevent their falling off, trim each end with a sharp knife, roast them gently, and froth and serve them up with a cullis sauce under

Breast of Veal with Oysters.

Cut off the under bone of a breast of white veal, and the skin from the top; then blanch and braise it, or roast it gently till very tender with a veal caul over. When it is to be served up take off the caul, glaize the top of the breast, and put round it white oyster sauce. (See receipt for *Oyster Sauce.*)

Lamb's Head minced.

Chop the head in halves, and blanch it with the liver, heart, and lights. Then chop the heart, &c. and add to them a little parsley chopped very fine, a small quantity of shredded lemon peel, and some cullis; then stew it gently till done, and season to the palate. Wash the head over with yolk of egg, season it with pepper and salt, strew fine breadcrumbs over, and bake it gently till very tender. When it is to be served up, colour it with a salamander, put the mince under, and the brains fried round it, with rashers of broiled bacon.

N. B. To prepare the brains, clean them in warm water, wipe them dry, dip them in yolk of egg, breadcrumb, and fry them in boiling lard.

Breast of Lamb with Benshamelle.

Take off the under bone, then blanch and put it into a stewpan, with parsley, thyme, and eschallots, chopped very fine, a bit of fresh butter, pepper, salt, a little essence of anchovie, and lemon juice. Let it simmer over a slow fire till nearly done; then lay it on a dish, and, when almost cool, egg and breadcrumb it, broil it over a slow clear fire till tender, and let it be of a nice brown colour. Serve it up with a benshamelle sauce under.

Breast or Tendrons of Lamb en Matelote.

Cut the breast into two long slips, trim off the bone and skin, cut them into small pieces, blanch and boil them in a little stock and lemon juice. When nearly done, add peeled and half-boiled button onions, pieces of pickle cucumber cut of the same size, a few button mushrooms stewed, some slices of throat sweetbreads, blanched omlet of egg (the same kind as for garnishing) cut into pieces the form of dice, and lean ham cut in the same manner; then add a cullis or benshamelle. When it is to be served up, put sippets of fried bread round.

Breast of Lamb with Peas.

Cut off the under bone, and then blanch and braise it. When it is to be served up, glaize the top and put the stewed peas under.

To stew Peas for Sauce: for Lamb, Veal, Chickens, &c.

To a quart of shelled young green peas add two ounces of fresh butter, a very little sifted sugar, and some salt. Put them into a stewpan, cover it close, simmer the peas till nearly done, then add some good-seasoned cullis, and stew them till tender.

Lamb Cutlets with Cucumbers.

Take the bone from a loin of lamb, cut it into chops, beat them flat with a chopper, and trim off some of the fat. Pass them with a piece of fresh butter, chopped parsley, thyme, eschallots, lemon juice, and pepper and salt. When three parts done, put them on a dish, and, when nearly cool, egg, breadcrumb, and fry them in boiling lard till of a light brown colour. Drain them dry, place them round each other in the dish, and serve them up with the cucumber sauce in the center.

N. B. In the same manner may be done mutton and veal cutlets.

Neck of Lamb glaized.

Cut the scragg and the chine bone from a neck of house lamb; then take off the skin, trim part of the fat away to lard the neck lengthways, blanch it, and braise or roast it gently with a veal caul over. When it is to be served up, glaize the larding, and put round it white onion sauce made thus:

Onion Sauce.

Take boiled onions, rub them through a hair sieve; then add to them fresh butter, cream, flour, salt, a very little of each, and let it stew five minutes.

Lamb Cutlets with Tendrons.

Cut a neck of house lamb into chops, leaving only the long bone; then beat them flat, and pass them with parsley, thyme, eschallots, chopped very fine, and add a little lemon juice, mushroom powder, pepper, and salt. When they are three parts done lay them on a dish, and when half cold breadcrumb them and broil them on a stewpan cover over a slow fire with a bit of fresh butter. When they are to be served up, put in the center of the dish some braised tendrons of the breast of lamb, and round them the cutlets, and turnip sauce over the center.

Turnip Sauce.

Pare four turnips, sweat them with a little water till they are done and the liquor reduced, then rub them through a tamis sieve. Add to them a small quantity of benshamelle, and then cut some more turnips in shapes as for a haricot. Sweat them in the like manner, and add the benshamelle to them.

Lamb Cutlets with Tendrons another way.

The tendrons may be served in the center of the dish, with the cutlets larded, braised, and glaized, to go round them; and the sauce made in the same manner, but instead of benshamelle add cullis.

Shoulder of Lamb glaized.

Bone a shoulder of house lamb, then season it with pepper, salt, mushroom powder, and beaten spice; fill the cavity with some light forcemeat; sew it up, and make it in the form of a leg of lamb; after which blanch it, and braise in a little stock and bards of fat bacon. When it is done wipe it dry, glaize it, and serve it up with sorrel sauce under; or a strong cullis sauce with a little tarragon of vinegar in it.

Shoulder of Lamb en Epigram.

ROAST a shoulder of lamb till three parts done, and let it stand till cold; then take the blade-bone out with the meat, leaving only the skin whole in the form of a fan. Cut the meat into slips, add to it parsley, thyme, eschallots, and mushrooms, chopped fine, some good-seasoned cullis, and a little lemon pickle. Let it stew gently for a quarter of an hour; and let the fan of the shoulder and the blade bone be broiled, and served up over the stew.

Shoulder of Lamb grilled.

ROAST it till three parts done, then score it with chequers, season with pepper and salt, and grill it gently till done. Let it be of a light brown colour, and serve it up with a sauce over it made with cullis, ketchup, lemon juice, and a bit of fresh butter.

Hind Quarter of Lamb marinated.

BONE the leg, fill the cavity with a light forcemeat well-seasoned, sew it up and lard the top part of the quarter with slips of fat bacon. When done, take a quart of veal stock, half a gill of vinegar, whole black pepper, some salt, two bay leaves, three onions cut in pieces, a little garlick, and half a pint of rhenish wine. Boil all the ingredients together a quarter of an hour, put the lamb into a deep dish, and strain the liquor to it. Let it lay five or six hours, turn it several times, then roast the lamb gently with a veal caul over it. When it is nearly done, let it colour a little and glaize the top. Serve it up with a sauce under it, made with the above liquor boiled down almost to a glaize, with some cullis added.

N. B. In the same manner may be done a shoulder or leg of lamb.

Hind Quarter of Lamb with Spinach.

BOIL the leg, preserve it as white as possible, serve it up with spinach under, and the steaks round it very hot. The loin to be cut into chops, and seasoned with pepper and salt; then fried or broiled. Pick and boil the spinach till nearly done; then strain and squeeze it dry, chop it, and add a little piece of fresh butter, pepper, and salt, a little cullis or cream, and let it stew for five minutes.

N. B. The spinach may be served up as a dish with fried bread round it.

Leg of Lamb with Oysters.

BONE the leg, fill the cavity with light forcemeat, and some blanched and bearded oysters pounded with it. Sew it up, put over it slices of lemon, salt, bards of fat bacon, and paper. Roast it gently, and when it is to be served up, glaize it, and put a sauce round it made with oysters blanched and bearded, stewed mushrooms, boiled button onions, some cullis, and the oyster liquor they were blanched in. Season to the palate with cayenne and lemon juice.

Currie.

Cut two young chickens into pieces, and blanch and drain them dry; then put them into a stewpan with two table spoonfuls of currie powder and a gill of veal stock, and stew them gently till half done. Then cut into slices three middling-sized onions, and put them into a stewpan with a table spoonful of currie powder, a quart of veal stock, two ounces of jordan almonds blanched and pounded fine, and boil till the onions are tender; then rub it through a tamis sieve to the chicken, and season to the palate with cayenne pepper, salt, and lemon or tamarind juice. Let the chickens stew till three parts done, then pour the liquor into another stewpan, and add three ounces of fresh butter, a very little flour and water, and reduce it to three gills. Strain it through a tamis sieve to the chickens, and let them simmer till tender.

N. B. Rabbits may be done in the same manner.

Plain Rice to be eaten with Currie.

Pick one pound of rice, and wash it very clean; then have ready some boiling water and put the rice in. Let it simmer till three parts done, and strain and wash it in several waters till free from slime. Drain it in a large hair sieve, and when dry put it into a stewpan with some paper and the cover over it. Set it in a moderate oven for one hour and a half, or longer, if there be a greater quantity.

Currie of Lobster.

Boil lobsters till three parts done, and pick and cut the claws and tails into good-sized pieces; then add currie powder, and proceed with the same directions as with the chickens, only pound the body of the lobsters and spawn, if any, and add them to the almonds and other ingredients.

Currie of Veal.

Cut a piece of breast of veal into tendrons, and fry them in a little lard till of a light colour; then drain them dry, add currie powder, and proceed with the same directions as for chicken currie.

Currie of Mutton.

Take three pounds of the best end of a loin of mutton, cut off the bone and some of the fat; then cut the meat into small square pieces, fry them, and proceed with the same directions as for veal.

Pig's Head Currie.

Take a young porker's head, cleave it in half, blanch and wash it, then cut it into small thick pieces, fry them, and dress in the same manner as veal and mutton; only omit the fresh butter, as there will be a sufficient quantity of fat.

Directions for roasting.

Observe that in roasting it requires a good quick fire, but not too strong, and the meats should be well-jointed, trimmed neat, and covered with paper to preserve it from being too high a colour. Beef and mutton should not be done too much; veal, pork, and lamb, should be done well; and some little time before it is to be served up, take the paper off, sprinkle the meat with salt, and when of a proper colour, froth it with butter and flour. Large poultry to be papered and done in the same manner; but small poultry, such as chickens, woodcocks, rabbits, wild fowls, &c. will not require papering. The time the several articles will take roasting depends upon a little practice, as the weather and the different strengths of fires make a material alteration. I have given directions for some particular roasts which require a preparation; as for others which are served with sauces, they may be found under their respective heads: and for the trimmings of meat, &c. I have wrote a receipt to make into soup, or they may be put into the beef stock pot.

Soup for a Family.

Cut the particles of meat from the trimmings of different joints, as beef, mutton, veal, pork, &c. and when done put the bones into a pot, cover with water, and boil them till the goodness is extracted. Then strain the liquor, wash the trimmings of the vegetables, such as turnips, carrots, onions, leeks, celery, and a little cabbage. Cut all small, put them into a pot with the above liquor and some split peas; boil till the peas are tender, add a little dry mint, and rub it through a tamis cloth or sieve. Then season the meat with pepper and salt, sweated down till three parts tender, and add the pulp. Boil all together till the meat is done, skim it and serve it up with fried bread in the form of dice.

To prepare a Haunch of Venison, or Mutton, for roasting.

Take great care the venison is well hung and good. Wipe it, take the skin from the top part, and put butter and plenty of salt over it; then put paste confined on with four or five sheets of paper braced with packthread. Roast it gently, and ten minutes before it is done, take off the paper, let it colour gradually, and froth it with flour and butter. Serve up with the venison warm currant jelly in a boat, and some good gravy with a little red port in it in another sauce boat.

To roast Woodcocks or Snipes.

Take out the trail, then roast the birds, and ten minutes before they are done bake a toast, put the trail into a stewpan, with a little cullis and fresh butter, and boil them together. When the woodcocks are to be served up put the sauce over the toast, and the woodcocks upon it.

N. B. If the woodcocks are thin roast them with a bard of bacon over.

To roast Larks.

TAKE the entrails out of the birds, wash and wipe them dry, put them upon a lark spit, with small thin slices of fat bacon and a piece of a vine or green sage leaf between each, if approved; and while roasting, put over them crumbs of bread, or roast them plain. When they are done, serve them up with fried breadcrumbs round them, and melted butter in a sauce boat.

To fry Breadcrumbs.

RUB crumbs of bread through a hair sieve, have ready a clean frying pan, put them into it with a piece of fresh butter, set them over a moderate fire, keep stirring with a wooden spoon till they are of a light brown colour, and put them upon a plate.

Turkeys.

To be roasted with a stuffing in the breast, and served with bread sauce in a boat.

Rabbits.

To be roasted either plain, or a stuffing, with the liver chopped in it, put into the belly, and served up with parsley and butter in a boat.

Hares.

To be dressed in the same manner as rabbits, with stuffing; but served up with cullis and fresh butter put over, and warm currant jelly in a sauce boat.

Hare roasted another way.

STUFF as above, and while roasting drudge it with flour, baste it with milk, and so alternately till a quarter of an hour before the hare is done; then baste it with a quarter of a pound of fresh butter put into the dripping pan. Serve it up with a cullis sauce and butter put over, and currant jelly in a sauce boat.

N. B. Baste it repeatedly, as there must be a good crust over. It will require three pints of warm milk for that purpose.

Pigeons.

MAY be roasted with a little stuffing in them, or plain; and served up with parsley and butter.

Quails, or Ruffs and Rees.

To be roasted with bards of bacon and vine leaves over them, with sauce in a boat made with cullis and red port in it.

Guinea Fowls, Pea Fowls, Pullets, Chickens, and Turkey Poults.

To be roasted either larded or plain, and served up with gravy under, and bread and egg sauces in separate boats.

Wild Fowl.

To be roasted plain, not done too much, and served up with onion sauce in a boat; as also a small quantity of gravy and red port boiled together.

Partridges and Pheasants.

To be roasted plain, and served up with poivrade sauce hot, and bread sauce in boats.

Green Geese and Ducklings.

To be roasted with pepper and salt put in the bellies, and served with green sauce in a boat.

Other Geese and tame Ducks.

To be roasted with onion and sage chopped fine, seasoned with pepper and salt put into the inside, and served up with apple sauce in a boat.

To roast a Pig.

MAKE a stuffing with chopped sage, two eschallots, two eggs, breadcrumbs, and fresh butter, and season with pepper and salt; put it into the belly, sew it up, spit it, and rub it over with a paste brush dipped in sweet oil. Roast it gently, and when done cut off the head; then cut the body and the head in halves, lay them on a dish, put the stuffing with the brains into a stewpan, add to them some good gravy, make it boil, and serve up the pig with the sauce under it.

To roast Sweetbreads.

BLANCH heart sweetbreads till half done, then wash and wipe them dry, cut off some of the pipe, put yolk of eggs on the tops with a paste brush, and strew fine breadcrumbs over. Roast them gently till done and of a nice colour, serve them up with a toast under and melted butter poured over, together with some cullis sauce round.

To roast Ribs of Beef.

BONE the beef, roll it round like a fillet of veal, put a good stuffing in the center, bind it tight, roast it gently, and serve it up with brown oyster sauce round it.

Fillet of Veal.

To be done in the same manner as the above, with white oyster or cullis sauce round.

Observations on Meat and Poultry.

Meats to be preferred when of a good fatness and the lean appears juicy, but not particularly streaked with fat, as it then frequently happens to eat hard. When the season will permit let it hang for a week, and not more, as I have found that period bring it to its best state. Poultry, likewise, should be chosen tolerably fat and of a soft grain. Let them hang three or four days, which will add to their better eating; except woodcocks, snipes, larks, or pigs, which should be dressed fresh. Be particular that the poultry are trussed very neat.

Stuffing for Turkies, Hares, Veal, &c.

Chop very fine beef suet, parsley, thyme, eschallots, a very small quantity of marjoram, savory, basil, and lemon peel, with grated nutmeg, two eggs (or milk), pepper, salt, and an anchovie chopped (if approved). Mix all well together.

Gravy for Roast Meat, Steaks, and Poultry.

Cut slices of chuck beef, veal, and lean ham; pare onions, turnips, a carrot, and cut them with celery; then add a bunch of parsley and thyme, a few whole pepper, and a little mace. Put all the ingredients into a stewpan, set them over a moderate fire, sweat down till the liquor becomes of a light brown colour, and be careful not to let it burn. Discharge it with water or beef stock, season to the palate with salt, and, if required, add a little liquid of colour. Let it simmer till the meat is perfectly done, skim it free from fat, and strain it through a tamis cloth.

Peloe of Rice.

Wash, pick, and dress, in the same manner as the directions for plain rice, observing only, that, before it is to be set in the oven, add a little pounded mace with the rice; and put into a stewpan a chicken half boiled and a piece of pickle pork three parts boiled, and cover with the rice. When it is to be served up, put the fowl and pork at the bottom of the dish, the rice over, and garnish with boiled or fried button onions and halves of hard eggs, which should be hot.

Peloe of Rice another way.

Wash and pick two pounds of rice, boil it in plenty of water till half done, with a dozen of whole cardamum seeds; then drain it, pick out the seeds, put the rice into a stewpan, with three quarters of a pound of fresh butter and some pounded mace, and salt to the palate. Take a loin of house lamb or some fresh pork cut into small pieces; put them into a frying-pan, add cinnamon, cloves, cummin and cardamum seeds, a small quantity of each pounded and sifted, with a bit of butter and some cayenne pepper, and fry the meat till half done. Then take two bay leaves, four good-sized onions sliced, and add to them a pint and a half of veal stock. Boil them till tender and rub them through a tamis cloth or sieve; then boil the liquor over a fire till it is reduced to half a pint, add it to the fried meat and spices, together with some peeled button onions boiled. Then put some of the rice at the bottom of another stewpan, then a layer of meat and onions on the rice, and so on alternately till the whole is put in. Cover the pan close, set it in a moderately heated oven for two hours and a half, and when it is to be served up turn the rice out carefully on a dish.

Timbol of Rice.

PICK, wash, and parboil the rice; then strain it, put it into a stewpan with a little oiled butter and yolk of egg. Simmer it gently till tender; then fill an oval tin mould with the rice, press it down close, take the shape out of the mould, wash it lightly with a paste brush with yolk of egg, and set it in a quick oven. When it is a good colour cut a square piece out of the top, scoop out the inside, and fill the cavity with fricassee of chickens, or any thing else you please.

Petit Patties of Chicken and Ham.

SHEET the pans with puff paste, and put a bit of crumb of bread the bigness of a dice in each; then cover them with more paste, trim round the pan, wash the tops of the paste with egg, and bake the patties of a light colour. When they are to be served up take out the bread, have ready the white meat of dressed fowl, lean ham, an eschallot chopped fine, a spoonful of consumé of veal, a little cream, flour, salt, cayenne, and lemon juice, a small quantity of each. Mix all the ingredients together over a fire, boil them for five minutes, fill the patties with it, and serve them up very hot.

Patties of Lobsters or Oysters.

BAKE patties as before directed, fill them with lobsters or oysters chopped, add to them a little strong consumé of veal, a small quantity of flour, lemon juice, cayenne pepper, a bit of lemon peel, an eschallot chopped fine, an anchovie rubbed through a sieve, and mixed over a fire for five minutes.

N. B. The lobsters or oysters are to be half boiled before they are chopped.

Forcemeat Patties.

SHEET the pans as for chicken patties, but instead of bits of bread fill them with a light forcemeat well-seasoned. Cover and bake them, and serve them up with a little cullis added to the forcemeat.

Pulpton of Chicken, Rabbits, &c.

TAKE veal suet or beef marrow, chop it, put it into a stewpan over a fire till melted, and when lukewarm mix it to some flour with a little water into a paste. Knead it well, and rub fresh butter round the inside of a mould of any shape, and strew vermicelli upon the butter. Then sheet the mould over the vermicelli with the paste rolled of the thickness of half an inch, and within the paste put a layer of chicken, slices of sweetbread, mushrooms, artichoke bottoms, truffles, and morells; after which put a little light forcemeat round with a paste over, close it well, egg, and bake it gently. When to be served up, turn it out of the mould, make a little hole in the top, and put into it a good cullis.

N. B. Cut the chicken in pieces and blanch them; the sweetbreads, truffles, and morels to be blanched, and afterwards season with pepper and salt.

Fishmeagre Pie.

BONE and cut into pieces a male carp; make it into a forcemeat with some of the roe, parsley, thyme, eschallots chopped very fine, a quarter of a pound of fresh butter, pepper, salt, a little beaten spice, half a pint of cream, four eggs, and crumb of french bread. Afterwards take pieces of eel, salmon, and skate, pass them with sweet herbs, pepper, salt, lemon juice, and a bit of butter. When they are cold, put some of the forcemeat at the bottom of a deep dish, and mix with the fish some stewed mushrooms, button onions, truffles and morells blanched, and the roe cut into pieces, and put them into the dish with more forcemeat round the top; then cover with puff paste, ornament with leaves of paste, egg it, and bake it. When it is to be served up cut a small hole in the center of the top, and add a good cullis.

Raised Ham Pie, with Directions for making a raised Crust.

TAKE water boiling hot, put a piece of fresh butter into it, and mix it with flour into a paste, and as it gets cold knead it several times, taking care it is of a good consistence but not too stiff, and then raise it into any shape you please. Have ready part of a ham boiled till half done, trim it to the shape of the crust, which must be big enough to put some light forcemeat at the bottom and round the ham when in the pie. Cover it with the same kind of paste, pinch round the top, and egg and ornament it. Just before it is set in the oven add half a pint of madeira wine, bake it gently for four hours, and when it is to be served up add some good cullis, but be careful it is not too salt.

Raised Chicken Pie.

CUT chicken into pieces, and put them into a stewpan, either blanched or not, with a bit of fresh butter, lemon juice, pepper and salt, parsley, thyme, eschallots chopped very fine, and a little pounded mace. When the chicken are half done put them on a dish, and when cold raise the crust, put light forcemeat at the bottom, the chicken upon it, and more forcemeat round the top. Cover, bake gently, and when served up, cut off the lid, and add a ragout of sweetbreads, cocks combs, &c. &c.

N. B. Rabbits and veal may be done in the same manner; as also pigeons, but they are to be put into the crust whole.

Flat Chicken Pie (or Tourte).

CUT chicken into pieces, blanch them, and season with pepper and salt; then put a light forcemeat at the bottom of a deep dish, and upon it some of the chicken, some slices of throat sweetbreads seasoned, some stewed mushrooms, truffles and morells, and upon them the remainder of the chicken. Cover it with a puff paste, then egg and ornament the top with leaves of paste of the same kind, bake it of a nice colour, and when it is to be served up put into it a good cullis.

N. B. The chicken may be passed with sweet herbs, &c. and when cold put into the dish as above. Rabbits also may be done in the same manner.

Pigeon Pie.

WASH the pigeons in cold water and wipe them dry; then put into a deep dish a rump steak cut into pieces, beat with a chopper, and seasoned with pepper and salt, and upon it the pigeons with the liver, &c. seasoned. Add also some yolk of hard eggs, cover it with puff paste, egg and ornament it with small leaves, bake it, and add some cullis.

Raised Turkey Pie with a Tongue.

BONE a turkey, and have ready a boiled pickled tongue; pare the principal part, put it into the center of the turkey with some light forcemeat well-seasoned, and some slices of throat sweetbreads. Sew it up, and put it into boiling water for ten minutes. Then make a crust with raised paste big enough to receive the turkey, which, when cold, put in with bards of fat bacon upon it and forcemeat at the bottom of the crust; then cover and ornament it as a raised chicken pie, and bake it. When it is to be served up, take off the lid and the bards of bacon, glaize the breast lightly, and add a cullis or green truffle sauce.

N. B. Pullets, chickens, partridges, and pheasants, may be done in the same manner; but instead of the tongue put in whole green truffles pared, and some truffles pounded with the forcemeat, and when served up, add a good cullis. Or, instead of a raised crust, they may be put in a dish and covered with puff paste, &c.

Raised Macaroni Pie.

RAISE a crust and ornament and bake it, and when it is to be served up have ready some hot macaroni stewed and a white fricassee of chicken in separate stewpans. Put them alternately into the pie, strew a little grated parmezan cheese over it, put a slip of paper round the edge of the pie to prevent from burning, and colour the cheese with a salamander.

Raised Beef Steak Pie.

TAKE prime steaks of a rump of beef, cut the skin from the fat, beat the steaks with a chopper, cut them into middling-sized pieces, then pass them with a bit of fresh butter, pepper, salt, lemon juice, and eschallots chopped, and when they are half done put them into a dish till cold. Blanch oysters, strain them, and preserve the liquor; then raise a crust, put a layer of steak at the bottom, some oysters upon it, and so alternately; cover the pie, ornament and bake it. When it is to be served up put into it a good cullis, with the oyster liquor and some ketchup mixed with it.

N. B. In the same manner put steaks and oysters into a deep dish, and cover them with puff paste.

Veal Pie.

Cᴜᴛ the best end of a loin of veal into thin chops, take off part of the bone and some of the fat from the kidney, season with pepper and salt, put them into a deep dish with yolks of boiled eggs, cover with puff paste, egg and ornament with leaves, bake it, and when it is to be served up, put into it some good consumé.

Pork Pie.

Tᴀᴋᴇ a piece of loin of pork with the rind and part of the under bone cut off; then cut into chops, season them with pepper and salt, cover them with puff paste, bake the pie, and when it is to be served up put into it cullis, with the essence of two onions and a little mustard mixed with it.

N. B. I have directed puff paste to be used for meat pies, it having the best appearance when baked; but there is another mode which may be thought preferable; and which is, to mix together half a pound of sifted flour, six ounces of fresh butter, the yolks and whites of two eggs well beaten, and a little milk and salt; then knead it well.

Eel Pie.

Sᴋɪɴ and clean the eels, cut them into pieces of two inches long, pass them with chopped parsley and eschallots, a little grated nutmeg, pepper, salt, and lemon juice, for five minutes; then put a little light forcemeat at the bottom of a deep dish, put the eels over it, cover with puff paste, bake it, and put into it some benshamelle or cullis.

Mutton Pie.

Tᴀᴋᴇ off the bone from part of a loin of mutton, cut it into chops, and season with pepper and salt. Then put into a deep dish a layer of chops, and upon them some slices of peeled potatoes (and if approved, some thin slices of onions); put the remaining chops over, cover with puff paste, bake it, and add some cullis. Or, the chops may be passed with sweet herbs, &c. and when cold put into small or large raised crusts with the above vegetables, and when baked add some cullis.

Sea Pie.

Tᴀᴋᴇ small pieces of salt beef and pickle pork, veal and mutton chops, a goose or a duck cut into pieces, onions and potatoes cut into thick slices, and season with a little salt and plenty of pepper. Make a paste with beef suet chopped fine, some flour and water; knead them well together, then roll out the paste, sheet a large bowl with it, put into it the above ingredients alternately; cover it with the paste, put a cloth over, and boil four hours. When it is to be served up take off the cloth, make a little hole in the top, and add a good consumé.

Rissoles.

Cᴜᴛ into small slips breast of fowl, lean ham, pickle cucumbers, and anchovies; add to them consumé, cayenne pepper, breadcrumbs, and raw yolk of egg.

Simmer them over a fire for five minutes, and be careful not to let the mixture burn. Then put the mixture on a plate, and when cold, cut into pieces, and dip them in yolk of raw egg, afterwards in fine breadcrumbs, and mould them with the hands into what form you please. Have ready boiling lard, fry them of a nice colour, drain them dry, and serve them up with fried parsley under.

To fry Parsley.

TAKE fresh gathered parsley, pick, wash, and drain it very dry with a cloth. Have ready clean boiling lard, put the parsley into it, keep stirring with a skimmer, and when a little crisp, take it out, put it on a drainer, and strew salt over.

Puffs with Chicken, &c.

CHOP breast of fowl, lean ham, and half an anchovie; then add a small quantity of parsley, lemon peel, and eschallots, cut very fine, with a little cayenne and pounded mace. Put them into a stewpan with a ragout spoonful of benshamelle, set them over a fire for five minutes; then put the mixture on a plate, and when cold roll out puff paste thin, cut it into square pieces, put some of the mixture on them, fold the paste, run a jagger iron round to make them in form of a puff, fry them in boiling lard, and serve them up with fried parsley under.

Wings and Legs of Fowls with Colours.

CUT the legs from a good-sized fowl and the wings as large as possible, leaving no breast bone; then fill the cavities with light forcemeat, sew them up neat, blanch them, drain them dry, wash the tops with raw white of egg, and lay a small quantity of forcemeat on it, and work a sprig with slips of lean ham and white and yellow omlets of eggs. Then put them into a stewpan with a little stock, cover the pan close, and stew them gently till done and the liquor nearly reduced. When they are to be served up, put under a cullis boiled almost to a glaize.

N. B. They may be done in the same manner and served up cold; or put round them savory jelly, instead of cullis, for an ornamental supper.

Wings and Legs larded and glaized.

CUT the wings and legs and force them as before directed, then lard very neat and blanch them, and stew them with a little stock. When they are to be served up, glaize the larding, and put under a strong cullis, or sorrel sauce, or benshamelle.

N. B. They may be done likewise in the above manner, and served up cold for a ball supper.

Fowl a la Menehout.

TAKE the bones out of the legs and wings, and draw them in; then split the fowl from the top to the bottom of the back, skewer it down close, pass it with chopped parsley, thyme, and eschallots, pepper, salt, and lemon juice. When three parts done put it on a dish, and when cold wash it with yolk of egg with a paste brush, strew breadcrumbs over, and broil gently till done and of a light brown colour. Serve it up with a cullis sauce under, with ketchup and lemon-pickle mixed in it.

Pulled Chicken (or Turkey).

BOIL a fowl till three parts done, and let it stand till cold; then take off the skin, cut the white meat into slips, put them into a stewpan, add a little cream, a very small quantity of grated lemon-peel and pounded mace, cayenne, salt, one eschallot chopped, a little lemon juice, and a spoonful of consumé; thicken with a little flour and water, simmer it over a fire ten minutes, during which time score the legs and rump, season them with pepper and salt, broil them of a good colour, and serve them up over the pulled chicken.

Another Way.

CUT the fowl as above, and add to it some benshamelle; or, instead of thickening with flour and water as the above, add, five minutes before it is to be served up, a leason of two eggs.

Pullet a la Memorancy.

BONE it, leaving the legs and wings on; then season the inside with pepper, salt, and beaten spice. Put a light forcemeat into it, sew it up, truss it as for roasting, set it with hot water, lard it neat, and roast it gently with a veal caul over. When it is done, take off the caul, glaize the larding, and serve it up with white ragooed sweetbreads round it, or with strong cullis or plain benshamelle.

Chickens with Lemon Sauce.

BOIL two chickens as white as possible, or braise them with bards of bacon over them; and when they are done wipe them dry and pour the sauce over.

To make Lemon Sauce.

PARE two lemons and cut them into very small pieces in the form of dice; then take the liver and scalded parsley chopped, put them into a stewpan, add some boiling benshamelle and a little melted butter, and simmer over a fire for two minutes.

Fricassee of Chickens or Rabbits (white).

CUT them into pieces and blanch and drain them dry; then put them into a stewpan with a little veal stock, a blade of mace, and a middling-sized whole onion. Stew them gently till three parts done; then add slices of blanched throat sweetbreads, stewed white button mushrooms, egg balls, and pieces of artichoke bottoms. When they are all nearly stewed, season with salt and a little lemon juice, add a leason of three eggs, simmer it over a fire for five minutes, taking care not to let it curdle, and serve it up very hot, with the mace and onion taken out.

N. B. Instead of a leason, the stock it is stewed in may be almost reduced, and a benshamelle added with the sweetbreads, mushrooms, &c.

Chickens or Turkies with Celery.

BOIL or braise them, and when they are to be served up wipe them dry, and pour over them white celery sauce. Or they may be served with brown celery sauce under them, and the breast of the poultry glazed. [See *Celery Sauce, white and brown*.]

Turkies, Pullets, or Chickens, with Oyster Sauce.

BOIL them, wipe them dry, and when they are to be served up pour over them white oyster sauce.

To make white Oyster Sauce.

BLANCH large oysters till half done, and strain and preserve the liquor; then beard and wash them, and put the liquor, free from sediment, into a stewpan. Add to it two ounces of fresh butter, half a pint of good cream, a piece of lemon peel, and a blade of mace; put it over a fire, and when it nearly boils add mixed flour and water to thicken it properly. Season to the palate with lemon juice, salt, and a little cayenne pepper if approved; then strain it through a fine hair sieve to the oysters, and boil them gently five minutes.

N. B. In the same manner may be done stewed oysters for dishes, only serve them up with sippets of bread round.

Chickens with Peas.

TRUSS them as for boiling, blanch them five minutes, and wash them clean; then braise them till tender with a little veal stock and bards of fat bacon or with white paper over them. When they are to be served up wipe them dry, glaize the tops lightly, and put pea sauce under.

Another way to stew Chickens with Peas.

CUT the chickens into pieces, blanch and drain them dry, and put them into a stewpan with a little veal stock; then stew them till tender and the liquor almost reduced. When they are to be served up, put them on a dish, and the peas sauce over.

Fricassee of Chickens or Rabbits (brown).

CUT the chickens into pieces, and fry them in a little lard till of a light brown colour; then drain them with a cloth very dry; after which put them into a stewpan, add button mushrooms stewed, pieces of artichoke bottoms, blanched truffles, morells, egg balls, and some good-seasoned cullis. Set them over a moderate fire, stew them gently till done, and serve up with fried oysters round them.

To fry Oysters for a Dish.

OPEN twenty-four large oysters, blanch them with their own liquor, and when three parts done strain them, and preserve the liquor; then wash and let them drain. In the meanwhile make a batter with four table spoonfuls of flour, two eggs, a little pepper and salt, and their liquor. Beat it well with a wooden spoon or a whisk for five minutes. Put the oysters into the batter, mix them lightly, and have ready boiling lard. Take the oysters out singly with a fork, put them into the lard, and fry them of a nice brown colour. Then put them on a drainer, strew over a small quantity of salt, and serve them up. If they are for a dish put fried parsley under them, or stewed spinach.

Directions for Poultry, &c. plain boiled.

LET it be observed that turkies, chickens, and meats, intended to be plain boiled, should be soaked in cold water, and put afterwards into plenty of boiling pump water, kept skimmed and preserved as white as possible. The time they will take dressing depends on a little practice, as in roasting. Be particular in trimming the meats neat, and in trussing the poultry. The carving, likewise, should be carefully attended to, which is frequently expressed by the phrase of *cutting into pieces*.

Jugged Hare.

CASE the hare, cut off the shoulders and legs, and the back into three pieces. Daub them well with fat bacon, and put them into a stewpot with the trimmings. Add to them allspice, mace, whole pepper, a little of each; a small clove of garlick, three onions, two bay leaves, parsley, thyme, and savory, tied together in a small bunch; a quart of veal stock, three gills of red port; and simmer them over a fire till three parts done. Then take out the shoulders, legs, and back; put them into another stewpan, strain the liquor to them, and add some passed flour and butter to thicken it a little. Let it stew till tender, skim it free from fat, season with cayenne, salt, and lemon juice, and serve it up in a deep dish.

Glaized Hare.

CASE the hare, bone it as whole as possible, wash it, and fill the inside with light forcemeat; then sew it up, and truss it as for roasting. Lard the back with bacon, the same as a fricando veal; cover it with a veal caul, and roast it very gently. When it is to be served up, take off the caul, glaize the larding, and put strong cullis, with a gill of red port boiled with it, under the hare.

Duck aux Naves.

BONE a tame duck as whole as possible, and season the inside with beaten spices, pepper, and salt; then draw in the legs and wings, and fill the inside with light forcemeat. Sew it up, braise it in a pint of veal stock, cover it with white paper and the cover of the stewpan. Let it stew gently till tender, and the liquor almost reduced. When it is to be served up glaize the breast, and pour the sauce round it, which is to be made with turnips cut into shapes as for haricot; afterwards to be put into a stewpan and sweated with a bit of fresh butter till three parts done; then add a good cullis and the essence in which the duck was braised. When it boils, skim free from fat, season to the palate, and stew the turnips till done.

A Duck with Cucumbers.

THE duck to be boned, braised, and served up in the same manner as the above, but instead of turnips put cucumber sauce, or peas, as for veal tendrons.

A Duck a la Benshamelle.

BONE, braise, and glaize the duck as mentioned in the preceding article, and when it is to be served up put a sauce round it made with heads of sprue grass boiled in a little veal stock, and when tender rub them through a tamis. Add the pulp to a small quantity of benshamelle, boil them together for five minutes, and let the sauce be very white and strong.

Hashed Mutton for a Dish.

TAKE mutton ready dressed, cut it into thin slices, put them into a stewpan with slices of pickle cucumbers, or walnuts, or onions; then make a sauce with chopped eschallots or onions passed with a bit of fresh butter over a slow fire till three parts done; after which add a pint of veal stock, or gravy, and a little ketchup. Boil it ten minutes, season to the palate with cayenne pepper and salt; then strain it to the mutton, let it stew gently till thoroughly hot, and add a small quantity of liquid of colour.

N. B. In the same manner may be done beef; and when it is to be served up put the bones (which are to be seasoned with pepper and salt, and grilled) over the hash.

Hashed Venison.

TAKE the part least done of ready-dressed venison, cut it in slices, and put them into a stewpan; then pass a bit of fresh butter and flour and chopped eschallots over a slow fire for ten minutes, and add to them half a pint of red port, a pint and a half of veal stock, its own gravy, if any, a little piece of lemon peel, cayenne pepper, salt, and lemon juice. Season to the palate, boil all together a quarter of an hour, and strain it to the venison. Let it simmer gently till thoroughly hot.

N. B. The venison should not be put into the liquor above ten minutes before it is to be served up, by reason of the fat dissolving too much.

Hashed Fowls.

CUT into pieces (very neat) ready-dressed fowls, turkies, or rabbits, and put them into a stewpan; then make a thickening with a bit of fresh butter, flour, and chopped eschallots or onions mixed over a slow fire. Discharge it with veal stock, add a little lemon pickle and ketchup, season to the palate, put a small quantity of liquid of colour, boil for ten minutes, strain to the poultry, and let it stew gently. When served up, there may be put a few pieces of the fowl grilled round it.

N. B. Instead of the thickening and veal stock, may be added cullis with lemon pickle and ketchup.

Hashed Hare, Wild Fowl, Pheasants, or Partridges.

CUT the poultry into neat pieces, put them into a stewpan, and add a liquor made in the same manner as for venison; or put cullis and red port with their own gravy.

Broiled Beef Steaks.

TAKE a small fat rump of beef, and cut off the fillet and the first two or three steaks; then cut the remainder into steaks also, and cut the skin from the fat. Beat them with a chopper, and season with pepper and salt just before they are to be put on the gridiron, which should be well cleaned, and the steaks frequently turned. When they are done according to desire, serve them up on a hot dish with a little gravy under, some scraped horseradish, chopped eschallots, and pickles, on small plates, and oyster sauce in a sauce boat, or with slices of onions dipped in batter and fried.

N. B. The fillet and outside steaks of the rump may be made into a pudding, in order to have prime steaks for broiling.

Beef Steak Pudding.

TAKE flour, chopped suet, some milk, a little salt, and one egg, and mix them well together. Roll out the paste of half an inch thick, and sheet a bason or a bowl with it. Then trim the skin from the meat, beat the steaks well with a chopper, cut them into middling-sized pieces, season with pepper and salt, put them into the bason with blanched oysters and slices of potatoes alternately (or slices of onions, if approved). Cover the top with paste, and tie a cloth over the bason. Boil the pudding (if of a middling size) two hours; and when it is to be served up put into it a little cullis and ketchup.

Oyster Sauce for Beef Steaks.

BLANCH a pint of oysters, and preserve their liquor; then wash and beard them, and put their liquor into a stewpan with india soy and ketchup, a small quantity of each, and a quarter of a pound of fresh butter. Set them over a fire, and when nearly boiling thicken with flour and water; season to the palate with a little cayenne pepper, salt, and lemon juice; strain it to the oysters, and stew them gently five minutes.

To dress Mutton, Lamb, or Pork Chops in a plain Manner.

CUT a loin of mutton, lamb, or pork, into chops of a middling thickness; beat them with a chopper, trim off a sufficient quantity of the bone and fat; then season with pepper and salt, broil them over a clear moderate fire, and serve them up very hot with gravy.

N. B. Lamb chops may have stewed spinach or fried parsley underneath.

To dress Veal Cutlets.

Beat the cutlets with a chopper, and cut them into middling-sized pieces; then strew on each side of them a mixture of breadcrumbs, chopped parsley and thyme, grated nutmeg, pepper and salt, and broil them over a clear fire till done and of a nice colour. Serve them up with cullis sauce and ketchup in it, or stewed mushrooms and cullis. Rashers of broiled bacon and fried oysters (a few of each if approved) may be put round the cutlets or chops, which may be done in the same manner.

Minced Veal for a Dish.

Cut into small pieces ready dressed veal, put it into a stewpan, add to it a very small quantity of grated lemon peel and a little benshamelle; season to the palate with cayenne pepper, lemon juice, and salt; stew the veal gently ten minutes, and serve it up with sippets of bread round it either fried or plain.

Minced Veal another way.

Add to the veal a little stock, one eschallot chopped fine, some grated nutmeg and grated lemon peel, a very small quantity of each. Season with cayenne pepper, lemon juice, and salt. Let it stew ten minutes, and just before it is to be served up add a leason of two eggs and cream, simmer them together five minutes, and be careful it does not burn nor curdle. Sippets of bread, likewise, to be placed round.

Partridges or Pheasants au Choux.

Bone the birds, put into them some light forcemeat well-seasoned; sew them up, blanch and wipe them dry, and braise them in a pint of stock till tender. After which cut two savoys into quarters and boil them till a fourth part done; then squeeze them and tie round with twine, put them into a stewpan, add a pint of stock, and boil them gently till done. Then take the savoys out, cut off the strings, put the birds into the center of a dish, the savoys round them, and set the dish in an oven or in a warm place covered over. Then mix the two liquors together, season to the palate with pepper, salt, and lemon juice. Make it of a proper thickness with flour and water, boil it till three parts reduced, add a little colour and strain it. When the birds are to be served up glaize their breasts lightly, and put the sauce over the savoys.

Partridges or Pheasants with Truffles.

Bone the birds, and force and braise them in a small quantity of stock. When they are to be served up glaize the breasts lightly, and put green truffle sauce round them, with the essence of the birds mixed in it.

Turkey with Truffles.

Truss the turkey as for boiling, put some light forcemeat with truffles pounded with it into the cavity near the breast, and secure it from falling out. Then put slices of lemon, some salt, and bards of fat bacon on the breast, and white paper over it bound on with packthread, and roast gently (if a good-sized turkey) one hour and a half. When it is to be served up, take off the paper, glaize the breast, and put the truffle sauce round the turkey.

N. B. In the same manner may be done pullets or chickens.

Truffle Sauce for Turkies, &c.

Put green truffles into water, clean them well with a hard brush, cut the outside paring thinly off, trim them into shapes or round, put the trimmings into a marble mortar, pound them, and add to the forcemeat which is to be put into the cavity near the breast of the turkey. Then put the truffles into a stewpan with a pint of beef stock, stew them gently, and when the liquor is almost reduced add some cullis well-seasoned.

Turkey with Chesnuts.

Truss the turkey as for boiling, stuff it with light forcemeat and Spanish chesnuts whole, and paper and roast it as a turkey with truffles. When it is to be served up, glaize the breast and put chesnut sauce round it, made with good cullis and chesnuts, which should be boiled till half done, and then roasted in a frying pan till wholly done; after which let them be peeled and put into the cullis five minutes before the turkey is served up.

Turkey with Ragout.

Stuff it in the plain way, boil it, and when it is to be served up put over the following sauce:—Take slices of throat sweetbreads blanched, white button mushrooms stewed, artichoke bottoms boiled till half done and cut in halves, cocks combs boiled till done, a few egg balls scalded; add a good benshamelle, and stew them gently for ten minutes. Or, instead of benshamelle, there may be put to the above ingredients half a pint of veal stock, and let them all be boiled ten minutes; then add a leason of three eggs and cream, simmer them together five minutes more, and season with salt, lemon juice, and cayenne pepper.

Rabbits with Onions.

Boil them as white as possible, and when they are to be served up, wipe them dry and put over onion sauce, made thus:—Take mild onions peeled, and boiled till three parts done; then squeeze and chop them but not too small; add a bit of fresh butter, a little salt and flour, a sufficient quantity of cream to mix them, and a little white ground pepper, if approved. Let the sauce be of a good thickness, and simmered over a slow fire for ten minutes.

Glaized Sweetbreads.

Lard very neat two heart sweetbreads, then blanch and braise or roast them; and when they are to be served up, glaize the top part, and put stewed endive under them.

Matelote of Rabbits.

Cut them into pieces and blanch and wash them; then put them into a stew-pan with a gill of water, cover close and preserve them as white as possible. When they are nearly done and the liquor almost reduced, which should not be of any colour, add half a pint of good benshamelle, a few whole boiled cocks combs, pickle cucumbers, ham, tongue, omlets of eggs (the same as for garnishing) cut into small squares, and a few stewed button mushrooms. Stew them together for ten minutes, and serve the matelote up directly.

Sweetbreads en Erison.

To be done in the same manner as neck of veal, which see.

Stewed Giblets plain.

Cut two pair of scalded goose giblets into pieces of two inches long; then blanch them, trim the bones from the ends, and wash the giblets; after which drain them dry, put them into a stewpan with half a pint of stock, cover the pan close, simmer over a slow fire till three parts done and the liquor nearly reduced, then add good-seasoned cullis, and stew them till tender.

Stewed Giblets with Peas.

Proceed as with the above, except, instead of plain cullis, take a pint of shelled young green peas, and sweat them till three parts done with a bit of fresh butter and a little salt; then add some cullis, put them to the giblets, and stew them till tender. If requisite put a little liquid of colour.

Green Truffles for a Dish.

Well clean two pounds of green truffles; then put them into a stewpan with half a pint of stock, a gill of red port, and a little salt, and boil them gently half an hour. When they are to be served up, drain them dry and put them into a folded napkin. They are to be eaten with cold fresh butter, or with oil, vinegar, and cayenne pepper.

N. B. The liquor they were boiled in may be made into a cullis, and put into different sauces, such as haricot, ragout, or celery, &c.

Rabbits en Gallentine for a Dish.

Bone two rabbits, lay them flat, put a little light forcemeat upon them, and slips of lean ham, breast of fowl, and omlets of eggs white and yellow, the same as for garnishing. Roll the rabbits up tight and sew them, lard the top part with slips of fat bacon very neat, and blanch and braise them. When they are to be served up glaize the larding, and put good cullis under them.

Ham braised.

TAKE a mellow smoked ham perfectly clean; then well trim and put it into a braising pan; after which, add to it four quarts of water, a bottle of madeira wine, and a few bay leaves. Cover the pan close, and simmer the ham over a moderate fire till very tender. Then wipe it quite dry, take off the rind, glaize the top part, and serve it up on a large dish with stewed spinach on one side and mashed turnips on the other.

N. B. Hams may be plain boiled and served up in the same manner.

Pickled tongues may be stuffed with marrow and boiled, then peeled, and served up with the above vegetables and in the same manner.

Jerusalem Artichokes stewed.

PARE and cut them into halves, boil them in a little consumé till nearly done and the liquor almost reduced; then add a bit of fresh butter, salt, flour, and cream, a small quantity of each. Set them over a fire for five minutes, and serve them up with fried bread round.

Jerusalem Artichokes another way.

PARE and cut them into shapes as for haricot, and fry them in boiling-hot lard till of a light brown colour; then drain them dry, put them into a stewpan, and add a little strong cullis with a small quantity of vinegar and mustard mixed in it. Serve them up with fried bread round.

Mashed Potatoes.

PARE and steam or boil floury potatoes, and mash them with a wooden spoon; then add a bit of fresh butter, a little salt, and some milk or cream. Mix them well together over a fire for five minutes, then put them in the center of a dish, make them smooth, chequer the top with the back of a knife, and put some whole potatoes round if approved. Serve them up very hot, but be careful the mash is not too thin, and preserve them as white as possible.

N. B. The same mash may be put into scollop shells and coloured with a salamander; or the mash may be mixed with yolk of egg, then moulded with the hands into round balls, and fried in boiling lard.

Cauliflower with Parmezan Cheese.

CUT off the leaves and stalk, boil it in salt and water till nearly done, and drain till dry. Have ready a dish with fried bread dipped in white of raw egg, and put round the rim. Set the flower in the center of the dish, and pour over it a sauce made with boiling-hot benshamelle, and, three minutes before it is to be put over the cauliflower, add grated parmezan cheese.

Cauliflower a la Sauce.

BOIL the flower, and either serve it up whole or in pieces, placed round each other in a dish. The sauce over it to be boiling hot and of a good thickness, made with strong cullis, a little vinegar, and fresh butter mixed together.

N. B. Broccoli may be done in the same manner.

Cauliflower a la Cream.

BOIL the flower and pour over it the following sauce:—Take a gill of consumé and a table spoonful of vinegar, which put into a stewpan and set over a fire till hot, and five minutes before it is to be sent to table add a leason of two eggs and a gill of cream.

Stewed Artichoke Bottoms.

BOIL six artichokes till half done; then take the leaves and choke away, trim the bottoms neat with a knife, or cut them with a shape; after which put them into a stewpan, add half a pint of stock, a little salt and lemon juice, and boil them gently till done. When they are to be served up wipe them dry, put them in the center of a dish with fried bread round the rim, and a strong bright cullis over them, or benshamelle.

French Beans a la Cream for a Dish.

CUT young beans in slips, boil them in plenty of water and salt to preserve them green, and when they are done drain them dry. Then put into a stewpan two ounces of fresh butter, the yolks of three eggs beat up in a gill of cream, and set over a slow fire. When it is hot add a table spoonful of vinegar and the beans, simmer all together for five minutes, and keep stirring the beans with a wooden spoon to prevent the mixture from burning or curdling.

Stewed Cardoons.

CUT the heads in pieces, take off the outside skin, wash, and scald them; then put them into a stewpan, add a little stock to cover them, boil till three parts done and the liquor almost reduced, then add a small quantity of benshamelle and stew them gently till done. Serve them up with sippets of fried bread and stewed watercresses alternately round the rim of the dish, and the cardoons in the center. Or they may be done in the same manner with cullis instead of benshamelle.

Vegetables in a Mould.

SHEET the inside of an oval jelly or cake mould with bards of fat bacon; then put upright alternately round the inside of the bacon slips of cleaned turnips, carrots, pickle cucumbers, and celery and asparagus heads. Lay a forcemeat at the bottom and round the inside of the vegetables, filling the center with small pieces of veal or mutton passed with sweet herbs, pepper, salt, and lemon juice. Cover it with forcemeat, wash it with yolk of egg, and bake it. When it is to be served up turn it gently out of the mould into a deep dish, take off the bacon, make a little hole at the top, and add a small quantity of good cullis.

Broiled Mushrooms.

CLEAN with a knife fresh forced mushrooms, and wash and drain them dry. Then make a case with a sheet of writing paper, rub the inside well with fresh butter, and fill it with the mushrooms. Season them with pepper and salt, put them upon a baking plate over a slow fire, cover them with a stewpot cover with some fire upon it, and when the mushrooms are nearly dry, serve them up very hot.

Stewed Mushrooms (brown).

CLEAN with a knife a pottle of fresh forced mushrooms, put them into water, and when they are to be stewed take them out with the hands to avoid the sediment. Then put them into a stewpan with an ounce and an half of fresh butter, a little salt, and the juice of half a lemon. Cover the stewpan close, put it over a fire, and let the mushrooms boil for five minutes. Then thicken them with a little flour and water mixed, add a small quantity of liquid of colour, (some cayenne if approved,) and stew them gently for five minutes more.

Stewed Mushrooms (white).

LET the same process be followed as above; but instead of adding liquid of colour put to them a gill of good cream.

Mashed Turnips.

PARE and boil them till three parts done; then squeeze them between two plates, put them into a stewpan, add flour, fresh butter, cream, and salt, a little of each. Mix them well over a fire, stew them gently for five minutes, and preserve them as white as possible.

Potatoes creamed.

PARE good potatoes, cut them into quarters, trim them round, and put them into a stewpan. Boil them gently till half done, drain them dry, add to them cream, salt, and fresh butter, a small quantity of each, or some benshamelle. Stew them very gently till they are done, and be careful they do not break.

Stewed Watercresses.

PICK and wash twelve bunches of watercresses, boil them till half done, and drain and squeeze them dry; then chop and put them into a stewpan, add to them cullis, cream, salt, pepper, and flour, a little of each. Stew them gently ten minutes, and serve them up with fried bread round.

A neat Dish of Vegetables.

WASH a dish with white of raw egg, then make four divisions in it with fried bread, and put alternately in each the following vegetables:—in the first, stewed spinach; in the second, mashed turnips; in the third, mashed potatoes; and in the fourth, slices of carrots and some button onions blanched: afterwards stew them in a little cullis, and when they are put into the dish let the essence adhere to them: or in the fourth partition put pieces of cauliflower or heads of broccoli.

N. B. Instead of fried bread to make the divisions, may be used mashed potatoes and yolks of eggs mixed together, and put on a dish in as many partitions as approved; afterwards baked till of a nice colour, and served up with any kind of stewed vegetable alternately.

Vegetable Pie.

Cut celery heads two inches long, turnips and carrots into shapes, some peeled button onions or two Spanish onions, artichoke bottoms cut into quarters, pieces of cauliflowers or heads of broccoli, and heads of large asparagus. Let all the vegetables be washed clean; then boil each separately in a sufficient quantity of water to cover them, and as they get tender strain the liquor into one stewpan and put the vegetables into another. Then add to their essences half a pint of strong consumé, thicken it with flour and water, season to the palate with cayenne pepper, salt, and lemon juice; add also a little colour. Let it boil ten minutes and strain it to the vegetables; then simmer them together, and serve them up in a raised pie crust, or in a deep dish with a raised crust baked round it, of two inches high.

Fried Potatoes.

Pare and slice potatoes half an inch thick; then wipe them dry, flour, and put them into boiling hot lard or dripping, and fry them of a light brown colour. Then drain them dry, sprinkle a little salt over, and serve them up directly with melted butter in a sauce boat.

Fried Onions with Parmezan Cheese.

Pare six large mild onions, and cut them into round slices of half an inch thick. Then make a batter with flour, half a gill of cream, a little pepper, salt, and three eggs, beat up for ten minutes; after which add a quarter of a pound of parmezan cheese grated fine and mixed well together, to which add the onions. Have ready boiling lard; then take the slices of onions out of the batter with a fork singly, and fry them gently till done and of a nice brown colour. Drain them dry, and serve them up placed round each other. Melted butter with a little mustard in it to be served in a sauce boat.

Pickle Tongue forced.

Boil it till half done, then peel it, and cut a piece out of the under part from the center, and put it into a marble mortar. Then add three ounces of beef marrow, half a gill of cream, the yolk of two eggs, a few breadcrumbs, a little pepper, and a spoonful of madeira wine. Pound them well together, fill the cavity in the tongue with it, sew it up, cover it with a veal caul, and roast till tender, or boil it.

Stewed Endive.

TRIM off the green part of endive heads, wash and cut them into pieces, and scald them till half done; then squeeze, chop, and put them into a stewpan; add a small quantity of strong cullis, stew it till tender, and serve it up in a sauce boat, or it may be put under roast mutton.

Forced Cucumbers.

PARE fresh gathered cucumbers of a middling-size; then cut them into halves, take out the seeds with a knife, fill the cavity with forcemeat, and bind the two halves together with strong thread. Put them into a stewpan with vinegar, salt, and veal stock, a small quantity of each. Set them over a fire, simmer them till three parts done, and reduce the liquor; then add with it a strong cullis, put it to the cucumbers, and stew them gently till done.

To stew Peas for a Dish.

PUT a quart of fresh shelled young peas into a stewpan, add to them a quarter of a pound of fresh butter, a middling-sized onion sliced very fine, a cos or cabbage lettuce washed and cut into pieces, and a very little salt. Cover the pan close, put it over a moderate fire, and sweat the peas till half done. Make them of a proper thickness with flour and water, add a spoonful of essence of ham, season to the palate with cayenne pepper, and add a small lump of sugar if approved. Let the peas stew gently till tender, being careful not to let them burn.

Salad of Asparagus.

SCALE and cut off the heads of large asparagus, boil them till nearly done, strain, and put them into cold water for five minutes, and drain them dry; afterwards lay them in rows on a dish, put slices of lemon round the rim, and mix well together a little mustard, oil, vinegar, cayenne pepper, and salt, and put it over the asparagus just before they are to be eaten.

Asparagus Peas.

SCALE sprue grass, cut it into pieces the bigness of peas as far as the green part extends from the heads, and wash and put them into a stewpan. To a quart of grass peas add half a pint of hot water lightly salted, and boil them till three parts done; after which strain and preserve the liquor, which boil down till nearly reduced, and put to it three ounces of fresh butter, half a gill of cream, a little sifted sugar, flour, and water, sufficient to make it of a proper thickness; add the peas, stew them till tender, and serve them up with the top of a french roll toasted and buttered put under them in a dish.

Another way.

BOIL the peas in salt and water till nearly done, strain and put them into a stewpan, add to them a little sifted sugar, two ounces of fresh butter, a table spoonful of essence of ham, half a gill of cream, with two yolks of raw eggs beat up in it; stew them gently five minutes, and be careful they do not burn. Serve them up in the same manner as the above.

N. B. Large heads of asparagus may be done in the same manner whole.

Stewed Asparagus for Sauce.

SCALE sprue or large asparagus, then cut off the heads as far as they are eatable, boil them till nearly done, strain them, and pour cold water over to preserve them green. Then make (boiling) a good strong cullis, and put in the heads five minutes before the sauce is served up, which may be put over tendrons of veal, lamb, &c.

N. B. Some tops of sprue grass may be boiled in a little stock till tender, and rubbed through a tamis. The pulp to be put to the cullis before the heads are added.

Directions for Vegetables.

IT is necessary to remember, that in dressing vegetables of every kind, they should be gathered fresh, picked clean, trimmed or pared neatly, and washed in several waters. Those that are to be plain boiled should be put into plenty of boiling water and salt. If they are not to be used directly, when they are three parts done put them into cold water for five minutes, such as spinach, greens, cauliflowers, and broccoli, as it preserves their colour; and when they are to be served up put them again into boiling water till done, then drain them dry.

N. B. Potatoes and carrots are best steamed.

Pickled Oysters.

PUT two dozen of large oysters into a stewpan over a fire with their liquor only, and boil them five minutes; then strain the liquor into another stewpan, and add to it a bay leaf, a little cayenne pepper, salt, a gill and a half of vinegar, half a gill of ketchup, a blade of mace, a few allspice, and a bit of lemon peel. Boil it till three parts reduced, then beard and wash the oysters, put them to the pickle, and boil them together two minutes. When they are to be served up place the oysters in rows, and strain the liquor over them. Garnish the dish with slices of lemon or barberries.

Oyster Atlets.

BLANCH throat sweetbreads, and cut them into slices; then take rashers of bacon the bigness of the slices of the sweetbreads, and as many large oysters blanched as there are pieces of sweetbread and bacon. Put the whole into a stewpan with a bit of fresh butter, parsley, thyme, and eschallots, chopped very fine, pepper, salt, and lemon juice, a small quantity of each. Put them over a slow fire, and simmer them five minutes; then lay them on a dish, and when a little cool, put upon a small wooden or silver skewer a slice of sweetbread, a slice of bacon, and an oyster, and so alternately till the skewers are full; then put breadcrumbs over them, which should be rubbed through a hair sieve, and broil the atlets gently till done and of a light brown colour. Serve them up with a little cullis under them, together with the liquor from the blanched oysters reduced and added to it.

Scollop Oysters.

Blanch the oysters and strain them; then add to their liquor, which must be free from sediment, a good piece of fresh butter, a little pepper and salt, some lemon peel and grated nutmeg, a small quantity of each. Then beard and wash the oysters, add them to the ingredients, simmer them over a fire five minutes, and put the oysters into scollop shells with the liquor. If there be more than sufficient, boil it till nearly reduced and add it; then put fine breadcrumbs over, smooth them with a knife, bake or set them over a fire upon a gridiron for half an hour, and colour the top part with a salamander.

Oyster Loaves.

Take small french rasped rolls, and cut a little piece off the top part; then take the crumb entirely out, and afterwards fry the case and tops in boiling lard only till they are crisp and of a light colour. Drain them dry, keep them warm, and just before they are to be served up put oysters into them, done in the same manner as for scollops, with the top of the rolls over.

Ragout of Sweetbreads (brown).

Take throat sweetbreads blanched and cut into slices; morells blanched, cut into halves, and washed free from grit; some stewed mushrooms, egg balls, artichoke bottoms, or jerusalem artichokes, boiled till half done and cut into pieces; green truffles pared, cut into slices half an inch thick, and stewed in a little stock till it is nearly reduced; and cocks combs boiled till three parts done. Then mix all the ingredients together, add some cullis, stew them gently a quarter of an hour, and season to the palate.

Ragout of Sweetbreads (white).

Put into a stewpan some stewed mushrooms, egg balls, slices of blanched throat sweetbreads, cocks combs boiled till nearly done, and half a pint of consumé. Stew them ten minutes, then pour the liquor into another stewpan, and reduce it over a fire to one half the quantity. Beat up the yolks of two eggs, a gill of cream, a little salt, and strain them through a hair sieve to the sweetbreads, &c. then put them over a slow fire and let them simmer five minutes; or the above four articles may be put into a stewpan with some benshamelle only, and stewed till done.

Poached Eggs with Sorrel or Endive.

Take a slice of bread round a loaf, and cut it to cover three parts of the inside of a dish; then fry it in boiling lard till of a light colour, drain it dry, and lay it in a warm place. Then wash and chop sorrel, squeeze and put it into a stewpan with a bit of fresh butter, cayenne pepper, and a table spoonful of essence of ham; simmer it till done, thicken it with flour and water, boil it five minutes, butter the toast, poach the eggs, and drain them; then lay them over the bread, put the sorrel sauce round, and serve them up very hot.

Buttered Eggs.

BREAK twelve eggs into a stewpan, add a little parsley chopped fine, one anchovie picked and rubbed through a hair sieve, two table spoonfuls of consumé or essence of ham, a quarter of a pound of fresh butter made just warm, and a small quantity of cayenne pepper. Beat all together, set them over a fire, and keep stirring with a wooden spoon till they are of a good thickness, and to prevent their burning. Serve them up in a deep dish with a fresh toast under them.

Fried Eggs, &c.

TAKE slices of ham or rashers of bacon, and broil, drain, and put them into a deep plate. Have ready a little boiling lard in a stewpan, break the eggs into it, and when they are set, turn and fry them not more than two minutes. Then take them out with a skimmer, drain them, and serve them up very hot over the bacon or ham. Put a strong cullis, with a little mustard and vinegar (but no salt) in it, under them.

Eggs a la Trip.

BOIL the eggs gently five minutes, then peel, wash, and cut them in halves; put them into a stewpan, add a little warm strong benshamelle, and a small quantity of parsley chopped very fine. Simmer them over a fire a few minutes, and serve them up plain, or with fried oysters round them.

Omlet of Eggs.

BREAK ten eggs, add to them a little parsley and one eschallot chopped fine, one anchovie picked and rubbed through a hair sieve, a small quantity of grated ham, a little pepper, and mix them well together. Have ready an iron frying-pan, which has been prepared over a fire with a bit of butter burnt in it for some time, in order that the eggs might not adhere to the pan when turned out. Wipe the pan very clean and dry; put into it two ounces of fresh butter, and when hot put in the mixture of eggs; then stir it with a wooden spoon till it begins to thicken, mould it to one side of the pan, let it remain one minute to brown, put a stewpan cover over it, and turn it over into a dish, and if approved (which will be a good addition) pour round it a little strong cullis, and serve it up very hot.

There may be added also, a small quantity of boiled tops of asparagus or celery, some fowl, or oysters, or other ingredients, pounded and rubbed through a sieve, with a table spoonful of cream and one of ketchup. Then add the pulp to the eggs, beat them well together, and fry them as above. Or the mixture, instead of being fried, may be put over a fire and stirred till it begins to thicken; then put it on a toast, colour it with a hot salamander, and serve it up with a little cullis or benshamelle, or green truffle sauce underneath.

Fricassee of Tripe.

Cut the tripe into small slips, and boil in a little consumé till the liquor is nearly reduced; then add to it a leason, of two yolks of eggs and cream, a small quantity of salt, cayenne pepper, and chopped parsley. Simmer all together over a slow fire for five minutes, and serve it up immediately. Or instead of the leason, &c. a little benshamelle and chopped parsley may be added.

Lambs Tails and Ears.

Scald four tails and five ears very clean, and braise them in a pint of veal stock. When the tails are half done, take them out, egg and breadcrumb them over, and broil them gently. Let the ears be stewed till three parts done, and nearly reduce the liquor; then add cullis, stew them till tender, and serve them up with the sauce in the center of the dish, the tails round them, and a bunch of pickle barberries over each ear. Or the tails and ears may be stewed in a little stock till tender; then add a leason of eggs and cream, and serve them up with twelve heads of large asparagus cut three inches long, boiled till done, and put over plain. Let the heads be preserved as green as possible.

Curried Atlets.

Take slices of throat sweetbreads, and slices of veal or mutton of the same size; put them into a stewpan with a bit of fresh butter, a table spoonful of currie powder, the juice of half a lemon, and a little salt. Set them over a slow fire, and when they are half done add to them blanched and bearded oysters with their liquor free from sediment. Simmer all together five minutes, lay them on a dish, and when cold put them alternately on small wooden or silver skewers. Then dip them in the liquor, strew fine breadcrumbs on each side, broil them over a clear fire till of a brown colour, and serve them up with some currie sauce under them.

N. B. The slices of sweetbread, oysters, veal, and mutton, to be of an equal number.

To stew Maccaroni.

Boil a quarter of a pound of riband maccaroni in beef stock till nearly done; then strain it and add a gill of cream, two ounces of fresh butter, a table spoonful of the essence of ham, three ounces of grated parmezan cheese, and a little cayenne pepper and salt. Mix them over a fire for five minutes, then put it on a dish, strew grated parmezan cheese over it, smooth it with a knife, and colour with a very hot salamander.

Stewed Cheese.

Cut small into a stewpan cheshire and gloucester cheese, a quarter of a pound of each; then add a gill of lisbon wine, a table spoonful of water, and (if approved) a tea spoonful of mustard. Mix them over a fire till the cheese is dissolved; then have ready a cheese plate with a lighted lamp beneath, put the mixture in, and serve it up directly. Send with it some fresh toasted bread in a toast rack.

To prepare a Batter for frying the following different articles, being a sufficient quantity for one Dish.

Take four ounces of best flour sifted, a little salt and pepper, three eggs, and a gill of beer; beat them together with a wooden spoon or a whisk for ten minutes. Let it be of a good thickness to adhere to the different articles.

Fried Celery.

Cut celery heads three inches long, boil them till half done, wipe them dry, and add to the batter. Have ready boiling lard, take out the heads singly with a fork, fry them of a light colour, drain them dry, and serve them up with fried parsley under.

Fried Peths.

To be done, and served up in the same manner as the above.

Fried Sweetbreads.

Let some throat sweetbreads be blanched, then cut into slices, and served up in the like way.

Fried Artichoke Bottoms.

Let the chokes be boiled till the leaves can be taken away, then cut the bottoms into halves and fry them in batter as the beforementioned articles; then serve them up with melted butter in a sauce boat with a little ground white pepper in it.

Fried Tripe and Onions.

Cut the tripe into slips of four inches long and three inches wide, dip them in the batter and fry them. When it is to be served up put under it slices of onions cut one inch thick, and fry them in the same manner. Or, instead of slips of tripe, pieces of cowheel may be used; and let melted butter be sent in a sauce boat with a little mustard in it, and (if approved) a table spoonful of vinegar.

Hard Eggs fried.

Let the eggs be boiled five minutes; then peel, wipe them dry, cut them in halves, dip them in batter, and fry them of a light brown colour. Serve them up with stewed spinach under, with a little strong cullis and essence of ham mixed in it.

To dress a Lamb's Fry.

SCALD the fry till half done; then strain, wash, and wipe it dry; dip the pieces in yolks of eggs, and breadcrumb them; fry them in plenty of boiling lard, and serve them up with fried parsley underneath.

Another Way.

SCALD the fry as above, and instead of dipping them in egg fry them in a plain way with a piece of butter till they are of a light brown colour; then drain and sprinkle a little pepper and salt over, and serve them up with fried parsley underneath.

Puffs with Forcemeat of Vegetables.

PUT into a stewpan a little fat bacon cut small, the same quantity of lean veal, some parsley and eschallots chopped together, and season with pepper, salt, and beaten spice. Then add six french beans, twelve heads of asparagus, six mushrooms chopped, and a little lemon juice. Stew the ingredients gently for ten minutes, then put them into a marble mortar, add a little cream, breadcrumbs, and yolk of egg, pounded well together. Then roll out puff paste half an inch thick, cut it into square pieces, fill them with the forcemeat, fold them, run a jagger iron round to form them like a puff, and fry them in boiling lard. Let them be of a brown colour, and drain them dry; then serve them up with sauce under them, made with a little cullis, lemon pickle, and ketchup.

Rammequins.

PUT into a pan four ounces of grated parmezan cheese, two ounces of fresh butter just warm, two yolks of eggs, a little parsley and an eschallot chopped fine, one anchovie picked and rubbed through a hair sieve, some cream, pepper, and salt, a small quantity of each, and beat them well together with a wooden spoon. Then make paper cases of three inches long, two inches wide, and two inches deep, and fill them with the mixture. Then whisk the whites of two eggs to a solid froth, put a little over the mixture in each case, and bake them either in an oven, or on a baking plate over a fire with a stewpot cover over them. Serve them up as soon as they are done.

To dress part of a Wild Boar.

PUT into a braising pan fourteen pounds weight of the boar; add to it a bottle of red port, eight onions sliced, six bay leaves, cayenne pepper, salt, a few cloves, mace, allspice, and two quarts of veal stock. Stew it gently, and when tender take it out of the liquor, put it into a deep dish, and set it in an oven. Then strain the liquor, reduce it to one quart, thicken it a little with passed flour and butter, and season it to the palate with lemon pickle. Let it boil ten minutes, skim it clean, pour it over the meat, and serve it up.

Plovers Eggs, to be served up in different ways.

BOIL them twenty minutes, and when they are cold peel and wipe them dry;

then lay them in a dish and put chopped savory jelly round and between them, and slices of lemon and bunches of pickled barberries round the rim of the dish. Or they may be served up in ornamental paper or wax baskets, with pickled parsley under them, and either peeled or not. Or they may be sent to the table hot in a napkin.

Buttered Lobsters.

Boil two lobsters till half done; then take off the tails, cut the bodies in halves, pick out the meat, and leave the shells whole. Then break the tails and claws, cut the meat very small, put it into a stewpan with a table spoonful of the essence of ham, two ounces of fresh butter, consumé and cream half a gill of each, a little beaten mace, one eschallot and parsley chopped very fine, and a few breadcrumbs. Then mix all together over a fire for five minutes, season to the palate with cayenne pepper, salt, and lemon juice; fill the reserved shells with the mixture, strew fine breadcrumbs over, and bake them gently twenty minutes. When they are to be served up colour the crumbs with a salamander.

N. B. In the same manner may be done a pickled crab.

Meat Cake.

Cut the fillet from the inside of a rump of beef into small pieces, also lean veal, and pound them very fine in a marble mortar. Then add a little lemon juice, pepper, salt, chopped parsley, basil, thyme, mushrooms, savory, and eschallots, a small quantity of each; some beaten spices, and yolks of eggs a sufficient quantity to bind it. Then add and mix with your hands some fat bacon and lean of ham cut into the form of small dice. Have ready a stewpan or a mould lined with bards of fat bacon, fill it with the mixture, press it down, put on the top bay leaves and a little rhenish wine, cover it with bards of bacon, put it into a moderate oven, and bake it thoroughly. When it is cold turn it out of the mould, trim it clean, set it on a dish, put chopped savory jelly round it, and a small modelled figure on the top; or the whole of the cake may be modelled.

Collared Pig.

Bone the pig; then have ready some light forcemeat, slips of lean ham, pickled cucumbers, fat bacon, white meat of fowl, and omlet of eggs white and yellow. Season the inside of the pig with beaten spices; then lay on them the forcemeat, and on that the slips of the above different articles alternately; after which roll it up, put it into a cloth, tie each end, sew the middle part, put it into a stewpan with a sufficient quantity of stock to cover it, and stew it two hours and a half. Then take it out of the liquor, tie each end tighter, lay it between two boards, and put a weight upon it to press it. When cold take it out of the cloth, trim and serve it up whole, either modelled or plain, or cut into slices, and put chopped savory jelly round.

N. B. In the same manner may be done a breast of veal, or a large fowl.

Red Beef for Slices.

TAKE a piece of thin flank of beef, and cut off the skin; then rub it well with a mixture made with two pounds of common salt, two ounces of bay salt, two ounces of salt petre, and half a pound of moist sugar, pounded in a marble mortar. Put it into an earthen pan, and turn and rub it every day for a week; then take it out of the brine, wipe it, and strew over pounded mace, cloves, pepper, a little allspice, and plenty of chopped parsley and a few eschallots. Then roll it up, bind it round with tape, boil it till tender, press it in like manner as collared pig, and when it is cold, cut into slices, and garnish with pickled barberries.

Savory Jelly.

TAKE the liquor, when cold, that either poultry or meat was braised in, or some veal stock, taking care it be very free from fat. Make it warm, and strain it through a tamis sieve into a clean stewpan; then season it to the palate with salt, lemon pickle, cayenne pepper, and tarragon or plain vinegar. Add a sufficient quantity of dissolved isinglass to make it of a proper stiffness, and whisk into it plenty of whites of eggs, a small quantity of the yolks and shells, and add a little liquid of colour. Then set it over a fire, and when it boils let it simmer a quarter of an hour, and run it through a jelly bag several times till perfectly bright.

Aspect of Fish.

PUT into a plain tin or copper mould warm savory jelly about an inch and an half deep; then take fresh smelts turned round, boil them gently in strong salt and water till done, and lay them on a drainer. When the savory jelly in the mould is quite cold, put the smelts upon it with the best side downwards; then put a little more jelly just lukewarm over the fish, and when that is cold fill the mould with more of the same kind. When it is to be served up dip the mould in warm water, put the dish upon the jelly, and turn it over.

N. B. Pieces of lobsters, fillets of soles, &c. may be done in the same manner.

Aspect of Meat or Fowl.

BONE either a shoulder of lamb or a fowl, and season the inside with pepper, salt, and a little beaten spice; then put into it some light forcemeat, sew it up, blanch, and then braise it in stock. When it is done lay it on a dish with the breast downward to preserve it as white as possible; and when the jelly which is in the mould is quite stiff, work on it a sprig or star with small slips of ham, pickle cucumber, breast of fowl, and omlets of egg white and yellow; then set it with a little jelly, and when cold put the meat or poultry upon it, and fill the mould with lukewarm jelly. When it is to be served up turn it out as the aspect of fish.

N. B. In the same manner may be done pieces of meat or poultry without forcing.

Canopies.

CUT some pieces of the crumb of bread about four inches long, three inches wide, and one inch thick, and fry them in boiling lard till of a light brown colour; then put them on a drainer, and cut into slips some breast of fowl, anchovies picked from the bone, pickle cucumbers, and ham or tongue. Then butter the pieces of bread on one side, and lay upon them alternately the different articles till filled. Trim the edges, and put the pieces (cut into what form you please) upon a dish with slices of lemon round the rim, and serve in a sauce boat a little mixture of oil, vinegar, cayenne pepper, and salt.

Solomongundy.

CHOP small and separately lean of boiled ham, breast of dressed fowl, picked anchovies, parsley, omlets of eggs white and yellow (the same kind as for garnishing), eshallots, a small quantity of pickle cucumbers, capers, and beet root. Then rub a saucer over with fresh butter, put it in the center of a dish, and make it secure from moving. Place round it in partitions the different articles separately till the saucer is covered, and put on the rim of the dish some slices of lemon.

Salad of Lobster.

TAKE boiled hen lobsters, break the shells, and preserve the meat as white as possible. Then cut the tails into halves, put them into the center of a dish with the red side upwards, and the meat of the claws whole. Then place round the lobster a row of parsley chopped fine, and a row of the spawn from the inside chopped, and afterwards mix a little of each and strew over the top of the lobster. Then put slices of lemon round the rim of the dish, and send in a sauce boat a mixture of oil, vinegar, mustard, cayenne pepper, and salt, a little of each.

French Salad

CONSISTS of the different herbs in season, as tarragon, chervil, sorrel, chives, endive, silician lettuces, watercresses, dandelion, beet root, celery, &c. all of which should be very young, fresh gathered, trimmed neat, washed clean, drained dry, and served up in a bowl. The sauce to be served up in a sauceboat, and to be made with oil, lemon pickle, vinegar, ketchup, cayenne pepper, a boiled yolk of an egg, and salt.

N. B. Some persons eat with this salad cold boiled turbot or other fish.

Blancmange.

To a quart of new milk add an ounce of picked isinglass, a small stick of cinnamon, a piece of lemon peel, a few coriander seeds washed, six bitter almonds blanched and pounded, or a laurel leaf. Put it over a fire, and when it boils simmer it till the isinglass is dissolved, and strain it through a tamis sieve into a bason. Let it stand ten minutes, skim it, pour it gently into another bason free from sediment, and when it begins to congeal stir it well and fill the shapes.

Dutch Blancmange.

PUT a pint of warm cleared calves feet jelly into a stewpan; mix with it the yolks of six eggs, set it over a fire, and whisk it till it begins to boil. Then set the pan in cold water and stir the mixture till nearly cold, to prevent it from curdling, and when it begins to thicken fill the shapes. When it is ready to be served up dip the shapes in warm water.

Riband Blancmange.

PUT into a shape some white blancmange two inches deep, and when it is quite cold put alternately, in the same manner, cleared calves feet jelly, white blancmange coloured with cochineal, or dutch blancmange.

Cleared Calves Feet Jelly.

TAKE scalded calves feet, chop them into pieces, put them into a pot with plenty of water to cover them, boil them gently four or five hours, strain the liquor, and preserve it till the next day in order that it may be quite stiff. Then take off the fat, and afterwards wash it with warm water to make it perfectly clean; after which put it into a stewpan, set it over a fire, and when it is dissolved season it well to the palate with lemon and seville orange juices, white wine and sugar, a piece of lemon peel, cinnamon, and coriander seeds whole, (or add a few drops of liquid of colour if thought requisite). Then whisk into it plenty of whites of eggs, a few yolks, and some shells. Let it boil gently a quarter of an hour, run it through a fine flannel bag several times till quite bright, and when it is nearly cold fill the shapes, which should be very clean and wiped dry.

N. B. When seville oranges are not in season, orange flower water may be added, or (if approved) syrup of roses or quinces. Old hock or madeira wine will make it of the best quality.

Marbrée Jelly.

PUT into a mould cleared calves feet jelly one inch deep, and when it is cold put on the center, with the ornamented side downwards, a medallion of wafer paper; or ripe fruits, such as, halves of peaches or nectarines of a fine colour, or black grapes; or small shapes of cold blancmange; or dried fruits, such as, cherries, barberries, green gages, &c. Then set them with a little lukewarm jelly, and when that is quite cold fill the mould with some nearly cold.

Bagnets a l'Eau.

TAKE half a pint of water, a stick of cinnamon, a bit of lemon peel, a gill of rhenish wine, and a few coriander seeds; sweeten to the palate with sugar, boil the ingredients ten minutes, add an ounce of fresh butter, and when it is melted strain the liquor to a sufficient quantity of flour to make it into a batter. Then put it over the fire again to simmer gently, and add six yolks of eggs. Have ready boiling lard, put into it pieces of the mixture of the bigness of a damson; fry them of a light brown colour, drain them, and serve them up with sifted sugar over.

N. B. The butter should be well beaten.

Apple Fritters for a Dish.

Mix together three ounces of sifted flour, a little salt, a gill of cream or milk, and three eggs; beat them for ten minutes with a spoon or whisk. Then pare twelve holland pippins, cut them into halves, core and put them into the batter. Have ready boiling lard, take the halves out singly with a fork, fry them till done and of a light colour, drain them dry, serve them up with sifted sugar over, some pounded cinnamon on one plate, and seville oranges on another.

N. B. Peaches or pears may be done in the same manner; or oranges, which are to be peeled, divided into quarters, and then put into the batter. Some jam likewise may be mixed with the batter instead of the apples, and fried in small pieces.

Golden Pippins a la Cream.

Take three gills of lisbon wine, a gill of water, a stick of cinnamon, a bit of lemon peel, a small quantity of the juice, and a few coriander seeds; sweeten well with lump sugar, and boil all together for ten minutes. Then have ready twelve large ripe golden pippins pared, and cored with a small iron apple scoop. Put them into a stewpan, strain the above liquor to them, and stew them gently till done; then take them out, put them into a trifle dish, and reduce the liquor to a strong syrup. After which mix with it a pint of cream, the yolks of ten eggs, and a dessert spoonful of syrup of cloves; then strain it, set it over a slow fire, and whisk till it is of a good thickness. Put the pan in cold water, stir the mixture some time, let it cool, and when the pippins are to be served up pour the cream over them, and put round the edge of the dish leaves of puff paste baked of a pale colour.

N. B. The same kind of cream may be put over codlins, gooseberries, or cranberries, when made into pies, only omitting the pippins.

Golden Pippins another way.

Take half a pint of white wine, a gill of water, a stick of cinnamon, a few cloves and coriander seeds, a bit of lemon peel, a little juice, and plenty of loaf sugar; boil them a quarter of an hour. Then strain the liquor to twelve large pippins pared and cored, stew them gently till done, and the liquor reduced to a strong syrup of a consistence sufficient to adhere to the apples, and put them into a dish. When cold serve them up with chopped cleared calves feet jelly round them.

Stewed Pippins another Way.

Proceed with the same ingredients as the preceding, but when the apples are half done lay them on a dish to cool, and add to the syrup the yolk of eight eggs and three gills of cream; then strain and set it over a fire, whisk it till of a good thickness, and let it stand till cold. Have ready boiling lard, dip the apples in batter of the same kind as for fritters, and fry them of a light colour; then drain them, and when cold serve them up with the cream under and sifted sugar over them.

Cream for Pies.

TAKE a pint of new milk; then add a few coriander seeds washed, a bit of lemon peel, a laurel leaf, a stick of cinnamon, four cloves, a blade of mace, some sugar, and boil all together ten minutes. Then have ready in another stewpan the yolks of six eggs and half a table spoonful of flour mixed, and strain the milk to them. Then set it over a slow fire, whisk it till it is of a good consistence, and be careful it does not curdle. When it is cold it may be put over green codlins, gooseberries, or currants, &c. in pies.

N. B. The cream may be perfumed, by adding, when nearly cold, a dessert spoonful of orange flower water, a table spoonful of syrup of roses, and a little ambergrise. Fruit pies, likewise, should be sweetened with sifted loaf sugar, covered with puff or tart paste, and when served up the top to be cut off, the fruit covered with either of the above creams, and small leaves of baked puff paste put round.

Mince Meat.

ROAST, with a paper over it, a fillet of beef cut from the inside of a rump, and when cold chop it small. To two pounds of meat add two pounds of beef suet chopped fine, two pounds of chopped apples, one pound of raisins stoned and chopped, one pound of currants washed and picked, half a pound of citron, a quarter of a pound of candied orange and a quarter of a pound of candied lemon peels cut into small slices; add some beaten cinnamon, mace, cloves, allspice, a small quantity of each, a pint of brandy, and a very little salt. Then mix all the ingredients well together, put them into a pan, and keep it close covered in a cool place.

N. B. It is advised that the meat be omitted, and instead of it add one pound of the yolks of hard eggs chopped.

Compote of Oranges.

PEEL and divide into quarters china oranges; then put them into a clear syrup, boil them gently five minutes, and take them out. Put into a gill of water a small quantity of cinnamon, cloves, and mace, the juice of two oranges, and a bit of the peel; boil them ten minutes, strain the liquor to the syrup, and reduce it to a strong consistence. Then put into it the quarters of the oranges, and when they are cold set them in a trifle dish, and put some cleared calves feet jelly chopped round them.

Tea Cream.

TAKE a pint of cream, a few coriander seeds washed, a stick of cinnamon, a bit of lemon peel, and sugar; boil them together for ten minutes; then add a gill of very strong green tea. Have ready the whites of six eggs beat up, and strain to them the cream; whisk it over a fire till it begins to thicken, then fill cups or a deep dish, and when cold garnish with whole ratafias.

Virgin Cream.

To be done in the same manner, only omitting the tea, and adding slices of citron when put into a dish.

Coffee Cream.

To be done in the same way, but instead of the liquid boil an ounce of whole coffee in the cream.

Burnt Cream.

To be done in the same manner as virgin cream, and when it is quite cold and to be served up put sifted sugar over, and burn it with a clear red-hot salamander. Put round the edge of the dish some ratafias.

Pastry Cream.

To a pint of cream add half a table spoonful of pounded cinnamon, a little grated lemon peel, three table spoonfuls of flour, two ounces of oiled fresh butter, eight yolks and the whites of three eggs well beaten, half a pound of sifted sugar, and a table spoonful of orange flower water. Put the ingredients over a fire, and when it begins to thicken add four ounces of ratafias and two ounces of pounded citron, mixing all well together. Let it stand till quite cold, then cut it into what shapes you please, and dip them singly into yolk of raw egg; then breadcrumb and fry them in boiling lard till of a light colour, drain them dry, and serve them up hot.

Almond Paste.

Blanch and pound very fine half a pound of jordan almonds, add six yolks of eggs, a sufficient quantity of flour to bind it well, an ounce of oiled fresh butter, and sweeten to the palate with sifted sugar. Mix the ingredients thoroughly in a marble mortar, and when it becomes a stiff paste roll it out, and cut it into what shapes you please; bake them, and when cold fill them with creams or jellies.

Cheese Cakes.

To three quarts of new milk add three parts of a gill of runnet; let it stand in a warm place, and when it is thoroughly turned drain it well, and mix into it with your hand half a pound of fresh butter, and sweeten to the palate with pounded sugar. Then add a few currants washed and picked, a little citron, candied orange and lemon peels cut into small slices, and an ounce of jordan almonds pounded fine. Then beat up three eggs, put them with the mixture, sheet the pans with puff paste, fill them with the curd, and bake them in a brisk oven. Or the paste may be made with half a pound of sifted flour, a quarter of a pound of fresh butter, and cold pump water, mixed lightly and rolled out.

Almond Nuts.

Take three eggs, their weight of sifted sugar, flour of the weight of two eggs, and two ounces of almonds blanched and pounded fine; then beat the whites to a solid froth, and mix the ingredients well with it. Have ready wafer or writing paper rubbed over with fresh butter, and with a teaspoon drop the mixture upon the paper in rows and bake them.

To make Syllabub.

To a pint and a half of cream add a pint of sweet wine, a gill of brandy, sifted sugar, and a little lemon juice; whisk it well, take off the froth with a spoon, lay it upon a large sieve, fill the glasses three parts full with the liquor, add a little grated nutmeg, and put the froth over.

Trifle.

Put into a deep china or glass dish half a pound of spunge biscuits, two ounces of ratafias, two ounces of jordan almonds blanched and pounded, citron and candied orange peel an ounce of each cut into small slices, some currant jelly and raspberry jam, a small quantity of grated nutmeg and lemon peel, half a pint of sweet wine, and a little of the liquor of the syllabub. Then make the same kind of cream as for pies, and when cold put it over the ingredients. When it is to be served up put plenty of the stiff froth of a syllabub raised high on the cream, and garnish with coloured comfits or rose leaves, which are recommended for elegance.

Tarts or Tartlets.

Sheet tart or tartlet pans with puff paste a quarter of an inch thick, trim round the edge with a sharp knife; then fill with raspberry or apricot jam, or orange marmalade or stewed apple, and put fine strings of paste across in what form you please. Bake them in a brisk oven, and be careful not to let the top colour too much.

Paste for stringing Tartlets.

Cut a bit of puff paste into pieces, mix with it half a handful of flour, a little cold water, and let it be of a moderate stiffness, and mould it with the hands till it draws into fine threads. Roll a piece out three inches long and two inches broad; then cut it into slips, draw them out singly, and put them across the tarts in any form, which may be repeated two or three times over each other, as it will add much to their appearance when baked.

To stew Apples for Tarts.

Pare, cut into quarters, and core, some apples; put them into a stewpan, add to them a piece of lemon peel, a little water, and a stick of cinnamon. Cover the pan close, put it over a fire till the apples are dissolved, sweeten to the palate with sifted sugar, add a table spoonful of syrup of cloves, and rub them through a hair sieve. Let it stand till cold before it is put into the paste.

N. B. To make a very fine flavoured tart, stew golden pippins in the same manner, and when they are rubbed through the sieve add only half a table spoonful of syrup of cloves, and mix well with it a quarter of a pound of pine-apple jam. This mixture will keep a month if close covered.

Fried Puffs with Sweetmeats.

ROLL out puff paste half an inch thick, cut it into slips of three inches wide, the slips into square pieces, and put on each some sweetmeat of any kind. Fold the paste, and run a jagger iron round to form it, or cut it with a sharp knife. Have ready boiling lard, fry them of a light colour, drain them dry, and serve them up with sifted sugar over.

Pyramid Paste.

TAKE a sheet of puff paste rolled of half an inch thick; cut or stamp it into oval forms, the first to be the size of the bottom of the dish in which it is to be served up, the second smaller, and so on till it becomes a pyramid; then put each piece separately on paper laid on a baking plate, and when the oven is ready, egg the top part of the pieces and bake them of a light colour. When they are done take them off the paper, lay them on a large dish till quite cold, and when to be served up set the largest piece in the dish for which it was formed, and put on it raspberry or apricot jams or currant jelly, the next size on that and more sweetmeats, proceeding in the same manner till all the pieces are placed on each other. Put dried fruits round the pyramid, such as green gages, barberries, or cherries.

N. B. Instead of stamping the pieces it is thought better to cut them with a sharp knife; then to cut out small pieces round the edges to make them appear like spires, as, being done in this manner, it causes the paste to appear lighter.

Iceing for a Cake.

WHISK the whites of four eggs to a solid froth, and put to it as much treble refined sifted sugar as you can; then add the juice of a lemon, mix all well together with a spoon, and spread it over the cake when warm.

Cherries in Brandy for Desserts.

ON a dry day gather the largest ripe morella cherries, and be careful they are not bruised; then cut off the stalk half way, prick each cherry with a needle four times, put them into glasses, add strong best brandy enough to cover them, and sweeten with clarified sugar. Tie over them a bladder washed and wiped dry, some white leather over that bound tight, and turn the glasses bottom upwards.

N. B. Grapes or apricots may be done in the same manner.

To make Buns.

PUT five pounds of best flour into a wooden bowl, set a spunge of it with a gill of yeast and a pint of warm milk; then mix with it one pound of sifted sugar, one pound of oiled fresh butter, coriander seeds, cinnamon, and mace, a small quantity of each pounded fine. Roll the paste into buns, set them on a baking plate rubbed over with a little butter, put them in a moderate oven to prove, then wash them with a paste brush dipped in warm milk, and bake them of a good colour.

Orgeat.

BLANCH a pound of jordan and one ounce of bitter almonds, pound them in a marble mortar till very fine; then put to them a pint of pump water, rub them through a tamis cloth till the almonds are quite dry, and add to the liquor more water to make it of a proper consistence for drinking; after which sweeten with clarified sugar, or sugarcandy, or capillaire; then put it into a decanter, and when it is to be used shake it together.

Orange Marmalade.

TAKE seville oranges when in season, which is generally at the beginning of March; cut them into halves, and the halves again into thin slices, which put with the juice, but not too much of the core, and take away the pips. To every pound weight of orange add two pounds of sifted sugar and a gill of water; then put them into a preserving pan, set the pan over a quick fire, and when the mixture boils keep stirring and skimming till it becomes of a proper stiffness, which may be known by putting a little into a saucer and setting it in cold water. Then fill the pots with the marmalade, and when cold put over white paper dipped in brandy; after which cover the pots with paper and white leather, and preserve them in a dry place for use.

N. B. In the same way try the proper stiffness of other jellies or jams, and cover them in like manner.

Raspberry Jam.

To every pound weight of ripe picked raspberries, add fourteen ounces of sifted sugar and half a gill of currant juice; put them into a preserving pan, set them over a brisk fire, and when it boils skim it well and let it simmer till it becomes of a good consistence.

N. B. The raspberries may be mashed with a spoon previous to adding the sugar, or rubbed through a wicker sieve.

Quince Jam.

PARE ripe quinces, cut them into thin slices, put them into a stewpan with a sufficient quantity of water to cover them, let them boil gently till tender close covered, and rub them through a large hair sieve; add to a pound of the pulp a pound and a half of sifted sugar and half a gill of syrup of cloves; then put them into a preserving pan, and let them simmer together till of a good strength.

N. B. A little of this jam mixed with apples in a pie will make it very good.

Green Guge Jam.

Rᴜʙ ripe gages through a large hair sieve, and put them into a preserving pan; then, to a pound of pulp add a pound of sifted sugar; after which boil to a proper thickness, skim it clean, and put it into small pots.

Apricot Jam.

Tᴀᴋᴇ apricots when nearly ripe, pare and cut them into halves, break the stones, blanch the kernels, and add them to the halves. To a pound of fruit put a pound of sifted sugar and a gill of the water in which the parings have been boiled. Then set it over a brisk fire, stir the mixture well together till it becomes of a good strength, but let it not be very stiff.

Preserved Apricots for Tarts or Desserts.

Cᴜᴛ ripe apricots in halves, blanch the kernels and add them to the fruit. Have ready clarified sugar boiling hot, put the apricots into it, and let them stand till cold. Then boil the syrup again, add the apricots as before, and when they are cold put the halves into small pots or glasses, and if the syrup is too thin boil it again, and when it is cold put it to the fruit, and cover it with paper dipped in brandy.

N. B. Green gages may be done whole in the same manner, or green gooseberries with the seeds taken out. These fruits may be served up with the syrup; or they may be dried on tin plates, in a moderately heated oven, and when almost cold put sifted sugar over.

Currant Jelly.

Tᴀᴋᴇ two thirds of ripe red currants and one third of white, pick them, put them into a preserving pan over a good fire, and when they are dissolved run their liquor through a flannel bag. To a pint of juice add fourteen ounces of sifted sugar. Set it over a brisk fire, let it boil quick, skim it clean, and reduce it to a good stiffness, which may be known as before directed in orange marmalade.

N. B. In the same manner may be made black currant jelly, but allowing sixteen ounces of sugar to a pint of juice.

Crisp Tart Paste.

Tᴀᴋᴇ half a pound of sifted flour, a quarter of a pound of fresh butter, two ounces of sifted sugar, and two eggs beaten; mix them with pump water, and knead the paste well.

Eggs and Bacon another way.

Bᴏɪʟ six eggs for five minutes, then peel and cut them into halves; after which take out the yolks, put them into a marble mortar with a small quantity of the white meat of dressed fowl, lean ham, a little chopped parsley, one eschallot, a table spoonful of cream, a dessert spoonful of ketchup, a little cayenne, some bread-crumbs, and sifted mace, a very small quantity of each. Pound all well together, fill the halves of the whites with the mixture, bake them gently ten minutes, and serve them up on rashers of bacon or ham broiled, and put some cullis over them.

To make Puff Paste.

MOULD with the hands a pound of fresh or good salt butter and lay it in cold water; then sift a pound of best white flour, rub lightly into it half the butter, mix it with cold spring water, roll it out, put on it (in pieces) half the remaining butter, fold the paste, roll it again, and add the remainder of the butter. Strew lightly upon it a little flour, fold it together, set it in a cold place, and when it is wanted for use, roll it out twice more.

N. B. In summer time the white of an egg beat up may be added with the water that mixes it.

To make an Almond Cake.

TAKE eight ounces of jordan and one ounce of bitter almonds, blanch and pound them very fine; then beat in with the almonds the yolks of eight eggs, and let the whites be whisked up to a solid froth. Then take eight table spoonfuls of sifted sugar, five spoonfuls of fine flour, a small quantity of grated lemon peel and pounded cinnamon, and mix all the ingredients. Rub the inside of a mould with fresh butter, fill it with the mixture, and bake it of a light colour.

Almond Custards.

ADD to a pint and a half of cream a small stick of cinnamon, a blade of mace, a bit of lemon peel, some nutmeg, and sugar to the palate. Boil the ingredients together ten minutes, and strain it; then blanch and pound (quite fine) three ounces of jordan and eight single bitter almonds; after which rub through a hair sieve, add the fine pulp to the cream, likewise a little syrup of roses, and the yolks of six eggs beat up, and put the mixture into small cups; or it may be baked in a dish with a rim of puff paste round it.

N. B. Plain custards may be made in the same manner, but instead of almonds add a little orange flower water.

Rhubarb Tart.

TAKE slips of green rhubarb, wash it, and cut it into small pieces the bigness of young gooseberries; put them into a dish, sweeten with sifted sugar, add the juice of a lemon, cover it with puff paste, and bake it. Serve it up either plain or with cream, the same as for an apple pie.

Orange Pudding.

PEEL four seville oranges thin, boil them till tender, rub them through a hair sieve, and preserve the fine pulp. Take a pound of naples biscuits, a little grated nutmeg, two ounces of fresh butter, and pour over them a quart of boiling milk or cream in which a stick of cinnamon has been boiled. When the ingredients are cold mix with them the pulp and eight eggs well beaten, sweeten to the palate, and (if approved) add half a gill of brandy. Edge a dish with puff paste, put in the mixture, garnish the top with strings of paste as for tartlets, and bake it in a moderately heated oven.

N. B. A lemon pudding may be made in the same manner.

Rice Pudding.

To a pint and a half of cream or new milk add a few coriander seeds, a bit of lemon peel, a stick of cinnamon, and sugar to the palate. Boil them together ten minutes, and strain it to two ounces of ground rice, which boil for ten minutes more. Let it stand till cold, and then put to it two ounces of oiled fresh butter, a little brandy, grated nutmeg, six eggs well beaten, and a gill of syrup of pippins. Mix all together, put it into a dish with puff paste round it, and bake it, taking care it is not done too much. Should the pudding be made with whole rice it should be boiled till nearly done before the cream is strained to it, and if approved a few currants may be added.

N. B. Millet or sago (whole or ground) may be done in the same manner.

Tansey Pudding.

BLANCH and pound very fine a quarter of a pound of jordan almonds; then put them into a stewpan, add a gill of the syrup of roses, the crumb of a french roll, a little grated nutmeg, half a gill of brandy, two table spoonfuls of tansey juice, three ounces of fresh butter, and some slices of citron. Pour over it a pint and a half of boiling cream or milk, sweeten to the palate, and when it is cold mix it well, add the juice of a lemon and eight eggs beaten. It may be either boiled or baked.

Almond Pudding.

To be made as a tansey pudding, only omitting the french bread and tansey juice, and adding as substitutes a quarter of a pound of naples biscuits and a spoonful of orange flower water.

Marrow Pudding.

BOIL with a quart of new milk cinnamon and lemon peel, and strain it to half a pound of beef marrow finely chopped, a few currants washed and picked, some slices of citron and orange peel candied, a little grated nutmeg, brandy, syrup of cloves, a table spoonful of each, and half a pound of naples biscuits. When the mixture is cold add eight eggs beat up, omitting five of the whites, and bake it in a dish with puff paste round it.

Bread Pudding.

To be made as a marrow pudding, only omitting the naples biscuits and a quarter of a pound of the beef marrow, adding as a substitute the crumb of french bread.

A rich Plum Pudding.

TAKE one pound of raisins stoned, one pound of currants washed and picked, one pound of beef suet chopped, two ounces of jordan almonds blanched and pounded, citron, candied orange and lemon peel pounded, two ounces of each, a little salt, some grated nutmeg and sugar, one pound of sifted flour, a gill of brandy, and eight eggs well beaten. Mix all together with cream or milk, and let it be of a good thickness; then tie it in a cloth, boil it five hours, and serve it up with melted butter over.

Batter Pudding.

To a pound of flour sifted add a little salt and a gill of milk, mix them till smooth, beat well six eggs, and add them together with more milk till the batter is of a proper thickness; then put the mixture into a bason rubbed with fresh butter, tie a cloth over, boil it an hour and a quarter, turn it out of the bason, and serve it up with melted butter, sugar, and grated nutmeg, in a sauce boat; to which may be added also (if approved) a table spoonful of white wine, or a dessert spoonful of vinegar.

N. B. When puddings are put into the pot the water in general should boil.

Boiled Apple Pudding.

MAKE a paste with flour, chopped beef suet, or marrow, a little salt and water; then knead it well, roll it out thin, sheet a bowl or bason with it, fill it with good baking apples pared, cut into quarters and cored; add lemon peel grated, cloves, nutmeg, and cinnamon pounded fine, a small quantity of each. Lay a thin paste on the top, tie the bason in a cloth, and let the pudding boil till well done. When it is to be served up cut a piece out of the top and mix with the apples, sugar to the palate, and add a bit of fresh butter and a little syrup of quinces.

Apple Dumplings.

PARE large baking apples, core them with a scoop, fill the cavities with quince marmalade, roll out (a quarter of an inch thick) the same kind of paste as for an apple pudding, mould over each apple a piece of paste, and boil them separately in a cloth, or wash them with whites of eggs with a paste brush, and bake them. Serve them up with grated nutmeg, sifted sugar, and fresh butter, in different saucers.

Baked Apple Pudding.

STEW the apples as for a tourte or tartlets, and when they are cold add to them six eggs well beaten; put the mixture into a dish with puff paste round the rim, and bake it.

Damson Pudding.

MAKE paste and sheet a bason in the same manner as for an apple pudding; then fill it with ripe or bottled damsons, cover it with paste, boil it, and when it is to be served up cut a piece out of the top, mix with the fruit, sifted sugar to the palate, and a small quantity of pounded cinnamon or grated nutmeg.

N. B. Puddings made with gooseberries, currants, or bullies, may be done in the same manner.

Damson Pudding another way.

To a pint of cream or milk add six eggs, four table spoonfuls of sifted flour, a very little salt, a small quantity of pounded cinnamon, and whisk them well together. Have ready ripe or bottled damsons, rub them through a hair sieve, add to the mixture a sufficient quantity of the fine pulp to make it in substance a little thicker than batter, sweeten it to the palate, put it into a buttered bason, flour a cloth and tie over, boil it an hour and a quarter, and when it is to be served up turn it out of the bason and put melted butter over.

N. B. In the same manner may be done ripe peaches, nectarines, gooseberries, apricots, green gages, or egg plums; or instead of boiling may be baked in a tart pan, sheeted with puff paste.

Baked Fruit Pudding another way.

Rub gooseberries or other ripe fruit through a hair sieve; and to half a pint of the fine pulp add a quarter of a pound of naples biscuits, three ounces of oiled fresh butter, half a pint of cream, grated nutmeg, sugar to the palate, and six eggs. Beat all the ingredients together for ten minutes; then add slices of citron, and bake the mixture in a dish with puff paste round the rim.

Muffin Pudding with dried Cherries.

To a pint and a half of milk add a few coriander seeds, a bit of lemon peel, sugar to the palate, and boil them together ten minutes. Then put four muffins into a pan, strain the milk over them, and, when they are cold, mash them with a wooden spoon; add half a gill of brandy, half a pound of dried cherries, a little grated nutmeg, two ounces of jordan almonds blanched and pounded very fine, and six eggs well beaten. Mix all together and boil in a bason, or bake it in a dish with paste round it.

Potatoe Pudding.

Peel potatoes, steam them, and rub them through a fine sieve. To half a pound of pulp add a quarter of a pound of fresh butter oiled, sifted sugar to the palate, half a gill of brandy, a little pounded cinnamon, half a pint of cream, a quarter of a pound of currants washed and picked, and eight eggs well beaten. Mix all together, bake (or boil) the pudding, and serve it up with melted butter in a sauceboat.

Carrot Pudding.

Take red carrots, boil them, cut off the red part, and rub them through a sieve or tamis cloth. To a quarter of a pound of pulp add half a pound of crumb of french bread, sifted sugar, a spoonful of orange flower water, half a pint of cream, some slices of candied citron, some grated nutmeg, a quarter of a pound of oiled fresh butter, eight eggs well beaten, and bake it in a dish with a paste round the rim.

Ice Cream.

TAKE a pint and a half of good cream, add to it half a pound of raspberry or other jams, or ripe fruits, and sifted sugar; mix them well together and rub through a fine sieve. Then put it into a freezing mould, set it in ice and salt, and stir it till it begins to congeal. After which put at the bottom of a mould white paper, fill with the cream, put more paper over, cover close, set it in ice till well frozen, and when it is to be turned out for table dip the mould in cold water. Or it may be served up in glasses, taking the cream out of the freezing mould.

Observation on Stores.

As frequent mention is made of syrups, jams, pounded spices, sugar sifted, grated nutmeg, and orange flower water, to be used in puddings and pies; and as a very small quantity of each is wanted at a time; it is therefore recommended (as a saving of trouble and expence) that the syrups, &c. be made when the fruits are in season, and preserved in small bottles with the different stores. But should any of the receipts be thought too expensive or rich, it is recommended, likewise, that a curtailment be made in some of the articles, pursuing nearly the same process, they being written in that state only to shew their first and best manner. The same observation may be borne in remembrance with respect to made dishes, roasting, pastry, or sauces.

Partridge Soup.

CUT to pieces two or three picked and drawn partridges or pheasants, an old fowl, a knuckle of veal, some lean ham, celeri, onions, turnips, a carrot, and a blade of mace. Put them into a stewpot with half a pint of water, set them over a fire close covered, and steam them till three parts done. Then add three quarts of beef stock, simmer till the ingredients are tender, strain the liquor through a fine sieve, and when cold take the fat clean off, add a little liquid of colour, a small quantity of salt and cayenne pepper, whisk with it two eggs and their shells, clear it over a good fire, and strain it through a tamis cloth; then cut half a middling-sized white cabbage into small slices, scald it, add to the soup, and boil it gently till tender.

Collared Eels.

SKIN and bone two large eels, lay them flat, and season with plenty of parsley, an eschallot chopped very fine, pepper, salt, beaten spices, and mushroom pow-der, a small quantity of each. Then roll and bind them tight with tape, put them into a stewpan with a pint of veal stock and a little lemon juice, simmer them over a fire till done, put them on a dish, skim the liquor free from fat, season with salt to the palate, clear it with two eggs, strain it through a tamis cloth, boil it down gently till of a strong jelly, and put it into a bason. When the eels are cold, take off the tape, trim the ends, wipe them dry, serve them up with the chopped jelly round them, a few bunches of pickled barberries on their tops, and slices of lemon round the rim of the dish.

N. B. Should the liquor be pale at the time it is cleared, add a few drops of liquid of colour.

White Puddings.

To half a pound of beef marrow chopped fine, add six ounces of jordan almonds blanched and pounded quite fine, with a dessert spoonful of orange flower water, half a pound of the crumb of french bread, half a pound of currants washed and picked, a quarter of a pound of sifted sugar, a little mace, cloves, and cinnamon pounded, a gill of mountain wine, and the yolks of four eggs beaten. Mix all well together, fill the entrails of a pig three parts full, tie each end, and boil them half an hour.

Sausage Meat.

TAKE the lean meat of young pork chopped small, and to a pound of it add a pound of the flay and fat chopped, some breadcrumbs, nutmeg, allspice and mace pounded, a small quantity of each, a little grated lemon peel, sage, parsley, thyme, and two eschallots, chopped very fine, an egg beaten, and season with pepper and salt. Mix all well together, with the hands, or pound it in a marble mortar; then make it into cakes and broil it, or put it into the entrails of a pig nicely cleaned.

Calf's Liver roasted.

MAKE an incision in the under part of a calf's liver, fill it with a stuffing made with beef marrow, breadcrumbs, grated nutmeg, one eschallot, two mushrooms, parsley and thyme chopped fine, and one egg beaten. Then sew it up, lard it with small slips of fat bacon, put a piece of veal caul over, and roast it gently. When it is to be served up take off the caul, glaize the top, put under it some good cullis sauce, and plenty of fried parsley round.

To dry Herbs.

GATHER marjoram, savory, thyme, basil, parsley, &c. on a dry day, when in season, and not blown. Divide them separately into small bunches, as in that state they will dry best. Then hang them on a line in a dry room or place where the air has free admission, but no direct rays of the sun. When they are perfectly dry (which will require two or three weeks to accomplish) put them in rows in boxes close covered, and set them in a dry place.

To make Anchovie Liquor to be used in Fish Sauces.

PUT into a stewpan one pound of best anchovies, two quarts of water, two bay leaves, some whole pepper, a little scraped horseradish, a sprig of thyme, two blades of mace, six eschallots chopped small, a gill of red port, half the rind of a lemon, a gill of ketchup; boil all together twenty minutes, and rub them through a tamis cloth with a wooden spoon. When the essence is cold put it into pint bottles, cork them close, and set them in a dry place.

Potted Lobster.

BOIL two live hen lobsters in strong salt and water till half done; then take the meat and spawn out of the shells, put it into a stewpan, add a little beaten and sifted mace, cloves, nutmeg, pepper, salt, a small quantity of lemon juice, a spoonful of essence of ham, a dessert spoonful of anchovie liquor, the same as for fish sauce, and simmer them over a fire for ten minutes. Then pound the meat in a marble mortar, reduce the liquor almost to a glaize, put it to the meat with a quarter of a pound of fresh butter, mix them well together, press the mixture down into small flat preserving pots, cover with clarified butter, and when cold put white paper over the pots, and set them in a dry place.

N. B. Prawns, shrimps, crayfish, and crabs, may be done in the same manner.

To clarify Butter for Potting.

PUT fresh butter into a stewpan with a spoonful of cold water, set it over a gentle fire till oiled, skim it, and let it stand till the sediment is settled; then pour off the oil, and when it begins to congeal put it over the different ingredients.

Potted Cheese.

To a pound of grated parmezan or cheshire cheese add three ounces of cold fresh butter, a little sifted mace, and a tea spoonful of mustard. Mix all well in a marble mortar, put it into small pots, cover with clarified butter, and set the pots in a cold dry place.

Potted Veal.

CUT small a pound of lean white veal, put it into a stewpan, with two ounces of fresh butter, the juice of a lemon, pepper, salt, sifted mace, a bay leaf, allspice, cloves, nutmeg, cinnamon, and mushroom powder, a small quantity of each, a little parsley, thyme, savory, and two eschallots chopped fine. Put them over a fire and stew them ten minutes; then pound them, and add a pound of the mellow part of a boiled pickle tongue and half a pound of cold fresh butter. Mix them well together with two eggs beaten; then press the mixture down tight into small pots, cover them with paper, put them into a moderate oven, bake them twenty minutes, and when the meat is cold put clarified butter over.

Potted Larks or Small Birds.

PASS them with the same ingredients as for veal, and when they are half done take them out and put the lean veal in. When the forcemeat is made put the birds into the pots with it, bake them, and proceed in the same manner as with potted veal.

N. B. Pheasants, partridges, chickens, &c. may be done in the same way, but will take a longer time baking.

To dry Morells, Mushrooms, and Champignons.

TAKE morells and champignons of the largest size, forced mushrooms of the size of a shilling, and let them be gathered fresh; then take off the stalk, wash them free from grit, drain them dry with a cloth, run a fine twine through them with a large needle, hang them up in a warm dry place, and when they are perfectly dry put them into paper bags in boxes close covered. When they are wanted for use lay them in warm water for half an hour, and prepare them as if they were fresh.

Mushroom Powder.

AFTER the mushrooms or champignons are dried whole they may be set before a fire till crisp; then grind and sift them through a fine sieve, and preserve the powder in small bottles close corked.

Potted Beef.

TAKE two pounds of the fillet out of the inside of a rump of beef and two pounds of best fat bacon. Cut them small, put them into a marble mortar, add to them a small quantity of parsley, thyme, savory, four eschallots chopped fine, some pepper, salt, two spoonsful of essence of ham, a spoonful of mushroom powder, sifted mace, cloves, and allspice, a little of each, two eggs beaten, and a gill of rhenish wine. Pound all well together till quite fine; then fill small pots with the mixture, cover with paper, bake it very gently for forty minutes, and when cold cover with clarified butter.

Tarragon Vinegar.

PUT into a stone jar half a pound of fresh gathered tarragon leaves and two quarts of best common vinegar, and let them ferment a fortnight; then run it through a flannel bag, and add to it a quarter of an ounce of isinglass dissolved in cyder. Put it into a clean jar, let it stand till fine, pour it off, put it into small bottles, cork them close, and set them in a dry place.

N. B. In the same manner may be done elder flowers, &c. &c.

Walnut Ketchup for Fish Sauces.

To a quart of walnut pickle add a quarter of a pound of anchovies and three gills of red port; boil them till reduced one third, strain it, and when cold preserve it in small bottles close corked.

To pickle Tongues, &c.

TAKE large tongues perfectly fresh, cut some of the root away, make an incision in the under part, rub them well with common salt, and lay them in a tub or pan close covered for four days. Then pound together two parts of saltpetre, one part of common salt, one part of bay salt, and one part of moist sugar. Rub the tongues well with the mixture, put all into the pan, and turn them every two days till pickled enough, which will be in ten days.

N. B. Pigs faces and hams to be done in the same manner, but according to their size let them lay in the different pickles for longer periods, and when well coloured smoke them. If it be wished to have the hams or tongues of a westphalia flavour add some socho to the pickle.

India Pickle.

TAKE large fresh cauliflowers in the month of July, pick them into small pieces, wash them clean, put them into a pan with plenty of salt over them for three days; then drain and lay them separately to dry in the sun, repeatedly turning them till they are almost of a brown colour, which will require several days. Then put plenty of whole ginger, slices of horseradish, peeled garlick, whole long pepper, peeled eschallots and onions, into salt and water for one night; drain and dry them also; and when the ingredients are ready, boil more than a sufficient quantity of vinegar to cover them, and to two quarts of it add an ounce of the best pale turmeric, and put the flowers and the other ingredients into stone jars, pour the vinegar boiling hot over, cover them till the next day, then boil the pickle again, and the same on the third day; after which fill the jars with liquor, cover them over close with bladder and white leather, and set them in a dry place.

N. B. In the same manner may be done white cabbages cut into half quarters, whole french beans, heads of celery, heads of asparagus, onions whole or sliced, or pickling melons peeled thin, cut into halves, and formed like an indian mango.

To dry Artichoke Bottoms.

GATHER the largest firm artichokes when in season, cut off the stalks, and boil them till the leaves and choke can be taken away. Afterwards put them on a baking plate and set them in a very slow heated oven, or hang them up in a warm place to dry, and when perfectly so put them into paper bags. When they are wanted for use lay them in warm water and salt, and when pliable trim them neat, braise them in stock and lemon juice, which will preserve them white, and when they are done enough, if for ragout, cut them into pieces; if for dishes, serve them whole with good cullis sauce over them.

To pickle Cucumbers, &c.

GATHER jerkins not too large, lay them in a strong brine of salt and water for three days, then wipe them dry, and put them into stone jars. Then put a sufficient quantity of vinegar to cover them into a preserving pan, add plenty of whole ginger and black pepper, a middling quantity of mace, allspice and cloves, some slices of horseradish, peeled onions, eschallots, and a small quantity of garlick. Let the ingredients boil for ten minutes, and pour them with the liquor over the cucumbers; cover the jars with cabbage leaves and a plate, set them in a warm place, the next day drain the liquor from them, boil it, and pour over them again, and if on the third day they are not green enough, boil the vinegar again, pour it over, and when cold tie bladder and white leather over the jars, and set them in a dry place.

N. B. In the same manner may be done walnuts, love apples, barberries, capsicums, french beans, nasturtiums, and small pickling melons peeled very thin and cut into quarters.

Rules to be observed in Pickling.

It is recommended that the best common vinegar be in general used for pickling, and that it be put into a well-cleaned copper or brass-preserving pan just before it is to be put over the fire, and when it boils not to remain in the pan.

There can be no occasion of the many arts that are used in order to preserve the ingredients green, if the vegetables are gathered fresh, on a dry day, when in season, and the process followed that has been recommended.

Further directions could be given that might be attended with greater expence, but which would scarcely answer a better purpose, excepting only to those who are in the habit of extensive practice.

To pickle Onions.

Peel small button onions into milk and water, in which put plenty of salt; set it over a fire, and when it boils strain the onions, wipe them dry, and put them into glasses. Have ready cold white wine vinegar, in which whole white pepper, ginger, mace, and slices of horseradish have been boiled. Pour it over the onions, and cover them with bladder and leather.

To pickle Mushrooms.

Take a sufficient quantity of double distilled white wine vinegar to cover the mushrooms; add to it whole white pepper, ginger, mace, peeled eschallots, and a small quantity of garlick if approved; boil all together ten minutes and let it stand till cold. Then peel fresh forced button mushrooms into water, wash them clean, strain, and put them into a stewpan. To a quart of mushrooms add the juice of a lemon and a table spoonful of salt. Cover the pan close, set it over a fire, and when the liquor is sufficiently drawn from the mushrooms put the whole into glasses and cover them with the pickle. Tie bladder and white leather over the glasses.

The general rule has been deviated from of making the pickle for onions and mushrooms with double distilled white wine vinegar, as in this instance it is requisite to preserve them white. It is likewise recommended that they be put into small jars or glasses for use; for this reason, that, if exposed to the air but for a short space of time, they will discolour.

To pickle Beet Roots.

Boil the roots till three parts done, and cut them into slices of an inch thick. Then take a sufficient quantity of vinegar to cover them, and add to it whole allspice, a few cloves, mace, black pepper, slices of horseradish, some onions, eschallots, a little pounded ginger, some salt, and a few bay leaves. Boil the ingredients together twenty minutes and strain it, and when the pickle is cold add a little bruised cochineal. Put the slices of beet into jars, add the pickle, put a small quantity of sweet oil on the top, and tie the jars down close.

N. B. When the beet is wanted for use mix well together sweet oil, mustard, some of the liquor in which the roots were pickled, and a very little sifted sugar. Lay the slices in a deep plate and pour the mixture over.

To pickle Artichoke Bottoms.

Take large fresh and sound artichokes, boil them just enough to take the leaves and choke away, then trim and lay them in salt and water; after which boil (for five minutes) a sufficient quantity of vinegar to cover them, in which put whole allspice, black pepper, ginger, mace, cloves, eschallots, salt, a few bay leaves, and some slices of horseradish. Drain and wipe dry the bottoms, put them into jars, add the liquor and ingredients to them, and tie them down close. When they are fit for use serve them up in a deep plate with a little of the pickle, oil, and mustard mixed with it.

To pickle large Cucumbers.

Peel them very thin, cut them into halves, throw the seeds away, and lay the cucumbers in salt for a day. Then wipe them dry, fill them with mustard seed, peeled eschallots, garlick, small slips of horseradish, and mace. After which tie them round with twine, put them into jars, pour over them some boiling liquor made as for india pickle or for jerkins, and cover them down close till fit for use.

To pickle Red Cabbage.

Cut a fresh light red cabbage into slips, wash it clean, and put it into a pan with plenty of salt for two days. Then boil together for half an hour a sufficient quantity of vinegar to cover the cabbage, together with bruised black pepper, mace, allspice, cloves, ginger, nutmeg, and mustard seed, a middling quantity of each. Strain the vinegar and ingredients, and let them stand till cold; then add a little bruised cochineal, drain the cabbage on a large sieve till dry, put it into the jars, add the pickle, and tie the jars down close; or the liquor may be poured over the cabbage boiling hot; and when cold, before the jars are tied down, add a little bruised cochineal. This method will make the cabbage sooner fit for use.

N. B. Onions may be peeled and done whole in the same manner, and mixed with red cabbage.

To pickle Currants.

To a quart of double distilled white wine vinegar add half a pound of loaf sugar, whole ginger, one ounce of salt, and a pint of red currant juice; boil all together, skim it clean, and let it stand till cold. Then pick and put some best ripe red currants into glasses, fill them with the pickle, and cover them down close with bladder and leather.

To pickle Barberries.

BRUISE and strain ripe barberries, and to a pint of juice add three pints of vinegar, a quarter of a pound of loaf sugar, an ounce of salt, and a quarter of an ounce of pounded and sifted ginger. Boil all together, skim it clean, and put bunches of the best ripe barberries into jars, pour the pickle boiling hot over, and let it stand till cold; then add a little bruised cochineal, and tie the jars over close.

N. B. Bunches of currants may be done in like manner.

Sour Crout.

TAKE large white cabbages when in season, cut them into halves, and then into slips; wash them clean and drain them dry. After which put into a tub a layer of cabbage, then a layer of salt, afterwards a small quantity of pounded and sifted coriander seeds, and so on alternately; when the tub is nearly full put a weight over to press it well, and set it in a cold dry place covered with a coarse cloth. When it is wanted for use put some of the cabbage into boiling water over a fire for five minutes, and strain it. Have ready some pieces of salted bouillie beef (of a quarter of a pound each) nearly boiled enough; likewise some pieces of pickle pork of the same number and weight. Then put them into a stewpan, add the cabbage, fresh butter, a little vinegar, onions sliced very thin, some whole pepper, allspice, and mace, tied in a bit of cloth. Let all stew till tender; then take out the spices, season the cabbage to the palate with cayenne pepper, and serve it up with fried onions (done as per receipt), with fried sausages round the crout.

Peas Pudding, to be eaten with boiled Pork.

LAY a pint of best split peas into water for half an hour; strain, pick, and put them into a cloth, tie them tight, and boil them gently for three hours. Then put the peas out of the cloth into a stewpan, mash them well with a wooden spoon, add a bit of fresh butter, a little pepper and salt, the yolks of two eggs, and mix all well together. Put the mixture into a clean cloth, tie it up, and let it hang near a fire for half an hour; then turn it out on a dish, and pour melted butter over.

Currie, or Pepper Water.

CUT a chicken into pieces, blanch and wash it, put it into a small stewpot, add a table spoonful of currie powder, half a pint of veal broth, and simmer them till half done. Then peel and cut into thin slices two good sized onions, fry them with two ounces of fresh butter till nearly done and of a brown colour; then add them to the chicken, together with a pint of veal broth, half a bay leaf, the juice of half a lemon, two table spoonfuls of the juice of tamarinds, which are to be dissolved in boiling water and strained. Boil all together till the chicken is nearly done; then take it out, put it into another stewpan, rub the ingredients through a tamis sieve, and add it to the fowl with a table spoonful of flour and water to thicken it. Make it boil, season it well to the palate with cayenne pepper and salt, skim it clean, and serve it up in a bowl.

Grills and Sauce, which are generally eaten after Dinner.

SEASON some small pieces of ready-dressed fowl or turkey with pepper and salt, and grill them gently till of a nice brown colour. In the mean time put into a stewpan a gill and a half of cullis, an ounce of fresh butter, a table spoonful of mushroom ketchup, the juice of a lemon, and a small bit of the rind, a little cayenne pepper, a tea spoonful of the essence of anchovies, and one eschallot chopped fine. Boil all the ingredients together five minutes, strain the liquor, and serve it up in a sauceboat; the pieces of chicken, &c. on a dish.

Salmé of Woodcocks.

TAKE two woodcocks half roasted, cut them up neatly, and let the trimmings with the entrails be pounded in a marble mortar; then put them into a stewpan, add half a pint of cullis, two eschallots chopped, half a gill of red port, and a bit of rind of lemon; season to the palate with pepper, salt, and lemon juice. Boil the ingredients ten minutes, and strain the liquor to the carved woodcocks, which stew gently till done. Serve them up in a deep dish with sippets of fried bread strewed over.

To make a Haggess.

TAKE the heart and lights of a sheep, and blanch and chop them; then add a pound of beef suet chopped very fine, crumb of french roll soaked in cream, a little beaten cinnamon, mace, cloves, and nutmeg, half a pint of sweet wine, a pound of raisins stoned and chopped, a sufficient quantity of flour to make it of a proper consistence, a little salt, the yolks of three eggs, and some sheep chitterlings well cleaned and cut into slips. Mix all together, and have ready a sheep's bag nicely cleaned, in which put the mixture; then tie it tight and boil it three hours.

French Black Puddings.

PICK, wash, and boil, till three parts done, two pounds of grits or rice; then drain it dry, put it into a stewpan with a quart of pigs blood preserved from curdling, with plenty of salt stirred into it when taken from the animal; add to them ground pepper, pounded and sifted mace, cloves, nutmeg, and allspice, a small quantity of each, a gill of cream with a bit of crumb of french bread soaked in it, together with chopped savory, thyme, parsley, and pennyroyal, a little of each. Mix the ingredients over a slow fire for twenty minutes, and when cold put with them plenty of the flay cut into small dice. Have ready the entrails cleaned very nice, fill them with the mixture three parts full, tie the ends, put the puddings into hot water, boil them gently a quarter of an hour; if they are to be eaten directly when done, prick them with a fork and broil them upon a very clean gridiron for ten minutes: if they are not to be eaten immediately when made, put them on clean straw, and when they are wanted for use put them into boiling water, let them simmer ten minutes, then take them out, and prick and broil them as above.

N. B. If large puddings they will take longer periods in boiling and broiling.

Milk Punch.

To a gallon of milk add a little cinnamon, cloves, mace, lemon and orange peel, a pint of brandy, a pint of rum, plenty of orange and lemon juice, and sweeten to the palate. Then whisk with it the yolks and whites of eight eggs, put it over a brisk fire, and when it boils let it simmer ten minutes; run it through a jelly bag till quite clear, put it into bottles, and cork it close.

N. B. The rum and brandy should be added when the milk is cleared.

Plum Pottage.

To veal and beef broths (a quart of each) add a pound of stoned pruens and the crumb of two penny french rolls, rubbing all through a tamis cloth; then mix to the pulp half a pound of stoned raisins, a quarter of a pound of currants, a little lemon juice, some pounded cinnamon, mace, and cloves, a pint of red port, a pint of claret, a small quantity of grated lemon peel, and season to the palate with lump sugar. Let all simmer together for one hour; then add a little cochineal to make it of a nice colour, and serve it up in a tureen. Let it be of the consistence of water gruel.

Candied Orange or Lemon Peels.

Take either lemon or orange peels well cleaned from the pulp, and lay them in salt and water for two days; then scald and drain them dry, put them into a thin syrup, and boil them till they look clear. After which take them out, and have ready a thick syrup made with fine loaf sugar; put them into it, and simmer till the sugar candies about the pan and peels. Then lay them separately on a hair sieve to drain, strew sifted sugar over, and set them to dry in a slow oven; or the peels may be cut into chips, and done in the same manner.

Lemonade or Orangeade.

To a gallon of spring water add some cinnamon and cloves, plenty of orange and lemon juices, with a bit of each peel; sweeten well with loaf sugar, and whisk with it the whites of six eggs and one yolk. Put it over a brisk fire, and when it boils let it simmer ten minutes; then run it through a jelly bag, and let it stand till cold before it is drunk. This mode is recommended, the liquor having been boiled.

Poivrade Sauce for Game, Maintenon Cutlets, &c.

Peel and chop small twelve eschallots; add to them a gill and a half of vinegar, a table spoonful of veal consumé, half an anchovie rubbed through a fine sieve, a little cayenne pepper, and salt. Serve it up in a sauceboat cold, if to be eaten with cold game; but if to be eaten with hot, roast, or grills, make it boiling.

Lobster Sauce for Fish.

Take the spawn out of live lobsters before they are boiled, bruise it well in a marble mortar, add a little cold water, strain it through a sieve and preserve it till wanted; then boil the lobsters, and when three parts done pick and cut the meat into small pieces, and put it into a stewpan. To the meat of a large lobster add a pound of fresh butter and a pint of water, including a sufficient quantity of the spawn liquor to colour it. Put it over a fire, thicken it with flour and water, keep stirring till it boils, and then season to the palate with anchovie liquor, lemon juice, and cayenne pepper. Let it simmer five minutes and skim it.

N. B. In place of the above the following method may be adopted:—Instead of cutting the meat of the lobster into pieces, it may be pounded in a marble mortar, then rubbed through a tamis cloth, and the pulp put with the other ingredients when the sauce is to be made. [See *Anchovie Essence for Fish Sauce.*]

Oyster Sauce for Fish.

BLANCH the oysters, strain them, and preserve their liquor; then wash and beard them, drain, and put them into a stewpan; then add fresh butter and the oyster liquor free from sediment, some flour and water to thicken it, season to the palate with lemon juice, anchovie liquor, a little cayenne pepper, a spoonful of ketchup if approved, and a bit of lemon peel. When it boils skim it, and let it simmer five minutes.

N. B. Muscles and cockles may be done in like manner.

Shrimp Sauce for Fish.

BOIL live shrimps in salt and water for three minutes, then pick, wash, and drain them dry; after which add fresh butter, water, anchovie liquor, lemon juice, cayenne pepper, and flour and water to make it of a sufficient thickness. Put the ingredients over a fire, and when it boils skim it, and let the shrimps simmer for five minutes. Or it may be made thus:—When the shrimps are picked, wash the shells, drain them dry, put them into a stewpan, add a little water, and boil them ten minutes; then strain the liquor to the butter (as above) instead of the water, which will make it of a better flavour. The bodies of lobsters, also, when picked, may be done in like manner for lobster sauce.

Dutch Sauce for Fish.

BOIL for five minutes, with a gill and a half of vinegar, a little scraped horse-radish; then strain it, and when it is cold add to it the yolks of two raw eggs, a quarter of a pound of fresh butter, a dessert spoonful of flour and water, and a little salt. Whisk the ingredients over a fire till the mixture almost boils, and serve it up directly to prevent it from curdling.

Anchovie Sauce for Fish.

PUT half a pound of fresh butter into a stewpan, add to it three spoonfuls of anchovie liquor, walnut and mushroom ketchups a spoonful of each, the juice of half a lemon, a little cayenne pepper, a tea spoonful of india soy if approved, a sufficient quantity of flour and water to make it of a proper thickness. Make the mixture boil, and skim it clean.

Observations in respect of Fish Sauces, &c.

Let it be particularly observed that fish sauces should be of the thickness of light batter, so that it might adhere to the fish when dressed, it being a frequent error that they are either too thick or too thin. The thickening should be made with the best white flour sifted, and some water, mixed smooth with a wooden spoon or a whisk, and to be of the consistence of light batter also. A little of it is recommended to be always ready where there is much cooking, as it is frequently wanted both in fish and other sauces.

There are, likewise, other articles repeatedly wanted for the use of stovework; and as their possession has been found to obviate much inconvenience and trouble, they are here enumerated: that is to say, liquid of colour preserved in a bottle, strained lemon juice preserved in the same manner, cayenne pepper, ground spices, ground pepper and salt mixed, which should be preserved separately in small jars; and every day, when wanted, fresh breadcrumbs rubbed through a hair sieve; parsley, thymes, eschallots, savoy, marjoram, and lemon peel, chopped very fine, and put on a dish in separate partitions.

Directions are not given for serving the fish sauces with any particular kind of fish,—such as turbot or salmon with lobster sauce, &c. but the receipts have been written only for the making them; therefore it is recommended that every person make a choice, and not be biassed altogether by custom.

Apple Sauce for Pork, Geese, &c.

Pare, quarter, and core, baking apples; put them into a stewpan, add a bit of lemon rind, a small stick of cinnamon, a few cloves, and a small quantity of water. Cover the pan close, set it over a moderate fire, and when the apples are tender take the peel and spices out; then add a bit of fresh butter, and sugar to the palate.

Green Sauce for Ducklings or Green Geese.

Pick green spinach or sorrel, wash it, and bruise it in a marble mortar, and strain the liquor through a tamis cloth. To a gill of the juice add a little loaf sugar, the yolk of a raw egg, and a spoonful of vinegar; if spinach juice, then put one ounce of fresh butter, and whisk all together over a fire till it begins to boil.

N. B. Should the sauce be made of spinach juice instead of vinegar, there may be put two table spoonfuls of the pulp of gooseberries rubbed through a hair sieve.

Fennel Sauce for Mackarel.

Pick green fennel, mint, and parsley, a little of each; wash, boil them till tender, drain and press them, chop them fine, add melted butter, and serve up the sauce immediately, for should the herbs be mixed with the butter any length of time before it is served up, they will be discoloured. The same observation should be noticed in making parsley and butter sauce.

Bread Sauce, for Turkies, Game, &c.

Soak a piece of crumb of bread with half a pint of milk or cream, add a peeled middling-sized onion, and put them over a fire; when the milk is absorbed bruise the bread, mix with it two ounces of fresh butter, a little white pepper, and salt; and when it is to be served up take out the onion.

Melted Butter.

In order to prevent butter from oiling, the flour and water that may be sufficient for the quantity of butter should be made boiling, skimmed clean, and the butter added to dissolve, being careful it is of a proper thickness.

In the same manner may be made fish sauces, adding the liquor of the lobsters or oysters, &c. with flour and water, and when boiling add the butter with the other ingredients.

To make Melon Citron.

Take middling-sized melons when half ripe, cut them in quarters, take away the seed, and lay the melons in salt and water for three days. Have ready a thin syrup; then drain and wipe dry the quarters, put them into the sugar, and let them simmer a quarter of an hour; the next day boil them up again, and so on for three days; then take them out, and add to the syrup some mountain wine, a little brandy, and more sugar; clarify it, and boil it nearly to a candied height, put the melons into it and boil them five minutes; then put them in glasses, and cover them close with bladder and leather.

Rusks, or Tops and Bottoms.

Take two eggs beat up, add them to a pint of good mild yest and a little milk. Sift four pounds of best white flour, and set a sponge with the above ingredients; then make boiling half a pound of fresh butter and some milk, a sufficient quantity to make the sponge the stiffness of common dough. Let it lay in the kneading trough till well risen; then mould and make it into the form of loaves of the bigness of small teacups; after which batch them flat, bake them in a moderate oven, and when nearly done take them out, cut the top from the bottom, and dry them till of a nice colour on tin plates in the oven.

Wafers.

Take a table spoonful of orange flower water, a table spoonful of flour, the same of good cream, sifted sugar to the palate, and a dessert spoonful of syrup of cinnamon; beat all the ingredients together for twenty minutes; then make the wafer tongs hot, and pour a little batter just sufficient to cover the irons; bake them over a slow fire, and when taken from the tongs roll them round, and preserve them in a dry place.

Cracknels.

To half a pound of best white flour sifted add half a pound of sifted loaf sugar, a quarter of a pound of fresh butter, two table spoonfuls of rose water, a little salt, the yolks and whites of three eggs beat up, and mix all well together for twenty minutes. Then roll it out, cut it into what shapes you please with a pastry cutter, put them on baking plates rubbed with butter, wash the tops of the paste with whites of eggs well beaten, and bake them in a brisk oven.

To bake Pears.

To a pint of water add the juice of three seville oranges, cinnamon, cloves, and mace, a small quantity of each, a bit of lemon peel, and boil them together a quarter of an hour; then strain and add to the liquor a pint of red port, plenty of loaf sugar, and a little cochineal; after which pare, cut into halves, and core, twelve large baking pears, put them into a pan, add the liquor, cover the pan with writing paper, and bake them in a moderate oven.

N. B. They may be done in the same manner in a stewpan over a fire.

To clarify Sugar.

To four pounds of loaf sugar put two quarts of water into a preserving pan, set it over a fire, and add (when it is warm) the whites of three eggs beat up with half a pint of water; when the syrup boils skim it clean, and let it simmer till perfectly clear.

N. B. To clarify sugar for carmel requires but a small quantity of water; and the different degrees of strength, when wanted, must be attended to with practice. They are generally thrown over a mould rubbed with sweet oil; for cakes, with a fork dipped in the sugar, &c.

Syrup of Cloves, &c.

PUT a quart of boiling water into a stewpan, add a quarter of a pound of cloves, cover the pan close, set it over a fire, and let the cloves boil gently for half an hour; then drain them dry, and add to a pint of the liquor two pounds of loaf sugar. Clear it with the whites of two eggs beat up with a little cold water, and let it simmer till it becomes a strong syrup. Preserve it in vials close corked.

N. B. In the same manner may be done cinnamon or mace.

Syrup of Golden Pippins.

TAKE the pippins when nearly ripe, pare, core, and cut them into very thin slices, or bruise them a little in a marble mortar. Then put them into an earthen vessel, add a small quantity of water, the rind of a lemon, plenty of sifted sugar, and a little lemon juice. Let the ingredients remain in the pan close covered for two days, then strain the juice through a piece of lawn, add more sugar if requisite, clear it with white of egg if necessary, and boil it to a syrup.

N. B. Nonpareils, quinces, pine-apples, or the rind of lemons peeled very thin, may be done in the same manner.

Syrup of Capillaire.

CLARIFY with three whites of egg four pounds of loaf sugar mixed with three quarts of spring water and a quarter of an ounce of isinglass; when it is cold add to the syrup a sufficient quantity of orange flower water as will make it palatable, and likewise a little syrup of cloves. Put it into bottles close corked for use.

Flowers in Sugar.

CLARIFY sugar to a carmel height, which may be known by dipping in a fork, and if it throws the sugar as fine as threads put in the flowers. Have ready teacups with the insides rubbed with sweet oil; put into each cup four silver table spoonfuls of the sugar and flowers, and when cold turn them out of the cups, and serve them up piled on each other.

Syrup of Roses.

GATHER one pound of damask rose leaves when in high season, put them into an earthen vessel, add a quart of boiling spring water, cover the pan close, and let it remain six hours; then run the liquor through a piece of lawn, and add to a pint of the juice a pound and a half of loaf sugar; boil it over a brisk fire till of a good syrup, being careful in the skimming, and preserve it in bottles close corked.

N. B. The syrup may be cleared with two eggs.

To preserve Cucumbers.

TAKE fresh gathered gerkins of a large size, and lay them in salt and water for two days; then drain and wipe them dry, put them into glasses, make boiling-hot a mixture of sugar, vinegar, and water, a small quantity of each; pour it over the cucumbers, cover and set them in a warm place, likewise boil the liquor and pour over them for three successive days. Then take a quart of the liquor, add to it plenty of cloves, mace, ginger, and lemon peel. Boil these ingredients for half an hour, strain and put to it plenty of sifted sugar, clear it with whites of eggs if requisite, boil to a strong syrup, and put it to the gerkins. When wiped dry and in the glasses, cover them down very close.

To preserve Currants.

TAKE large bunches of ripe currants, make a thin syrup with sugar and water, set it over a fire, when it boils put in the fruit, and let them remain in a cold place till the next day; then take them out carefully, lay them on a dish, make the liquor boil again, and put in the currants, taking care not to let them break. Take them out a second time, add more sugar to the syrup, with a quart of currant juice; clarify it, boil it to a strong syrup, and when it is cold put the currants into glasses, pour the syrup over, and tie them down close.

To preserve Barberries.

BRUISE a quart of ripe barberries, add a quart of spring water, put them over a fire, when boiling run the liquor through a fine sieve, and put with it three pounds of clarified sugar. Then add a sufficient quantity of large bunches of ripe barberries, put them over a fire, when boiling-hot set them away till the next day, take the barberries out of the syrup and put them into glasses; boil the liquor to a good consistence, pour it over, and cover them close.

Gooseberry Fool.

PUT a quart of green gooseberries and a gill of water in a stewpan over a fire close covered; when the fruit is tender rub it through a fine hair sieve, add to the pulp sifted loaf sugar, and let it stand till cold. In the mean time put a pint of cream or new milk into a stewpan, with a stick of cinnamon, a small piece of lemon peel, sugar, a few cloves and coriander seeds, and boil the ingredients ten minutes. Have ready the yolks of six eggs and a little flour and water well beaten; strain the milk to them, whisk it over a fire to prevent it from curdling, when it nearly boils set the pan in cold water, stir the cream for five minutes, and let it stand till cold. Then mix the pulp of the gooseberries and the cream together, add a little grated nutmeg, and sweeten it more if agreeable to the palate.

N. B. Strawberries, raspberries, apricots, and other ripe fruits, may be rubbed through a sieve and the pulp added to the cream.

Sago.

To half an ounce of sago washed clean add a pint of water and a bit of lemon peel; cover the pan close, set it over a fire, let it simmer till the sago is nearly done, and the liquor absorbed. Then put to it half a pint of red port, a tea spoonful of pounded cinnamon and cloves or mace, sweeten to the palate with loaf sugar, and let it boil gently for ten minutes.

Oatmeal Pottage, or Gruel.

MIX together three table spoonfuls of oatmeal, a very little salt, and a quart of water; put them over a fire, and let it boil gently for half an hour. Then skim and strain it, add to it an ounce of fresh butter, some loaf sugar, a little brandy, and grated nutmeg; or instead of these ingredients put pepper, salt, and fresh butter, to the palate; then boil it again five minutes, mix it till very smooth, and let it be of a moderate consistence.

To bottle Gooseberries, &c. for Tarts.

GATHER gooseberries on a dry day when about half grown, and pick off the stalks and blossoms; then put the fruit into wide-mouthed bottles and shake them down; cork them very close, bake them in a moderate oven till thoroughly heated through, and set them in a dry cool place.

N. B. Damsons, currants, cherries, or plums may be done in the same way.

[The above mode of preserving fruits is recommended in preference to preserving them with sugar, it frequently happening that fruits done with syrup will fret, and in that event the whole be spoiled.]

To bottle Gooseberries another way.

WHEN the gooseberries are picked put them into the bottles and cover them with spring water; then set them in a large pan of cold water, put them over a moderate fire, and when the gooseberries appear to be scalded enough take out the bottles and set them in a cool place, and when cold cork them close.

[This mode has been found to answer extremely well. The small champaign gooseberry is recommended likewise for the purpose.]

Small Cakes.

TAKE half a pound of sifted sugar, half a pound of fresh butter, three quarters of a pound of sifted flour, and rub all together; then wet it with a gill of boiling milk, strew in a few carraway seeds, and let it lay till the next day; after which mould and cut it into eleven dozen pieces, roll them as thin as possible, and bake them in an oven three parts cold.

Diet Bread Cake.

TAKE nine eggs and sifted sugar of their weight; break the whites into one pan and the yolks into another; then whisk the whites till of a solid froth, beat the yolks, and whisk them with the whites; add the sugar with the weight of five eggs of flour, mix all well together, put in a few carraway seeds, and bake it in a hoop.

Sponge Biscuits.

TAKE the same mixture as for diet bread, only omitting the carraway seeds; then rub the inside of small tin pans with fresh butter, fill them with the mixture, sift sugar over, and bake them in a moderate oven.

Common Seed Cake.

To one pound and a half of flour put half a pound of fresh butter broke into small pieces round it, likewise a quarter of a pound of sifted sugar, and half a grated nutmeg; then make a cavity in the center of the flour and set a sponge with a gill of yest and a little warm milk; when well risen add slices of candied orange or lemon peel and an egg beat up. Mix all these ingredients well together with a little warm milk, let the dough be of a proper stiffness, mould it into a cake, prove it in a warm place, and then bake it.

Cinnamon Cakes.

BREAK six eggs into a pan with three table spoonfuls of rose water, whisk them well together, add a pound of sifted sugar, a dessert spoonful of pounded cinnamon, and as much flour as will make it into a good paste; then roll it out, cut it into what shapes you please, bake them on white paper, and when done take them off, and preserve them in a dry place for use.

To make red Colouring for Pippin Paste, &c. for garnishing Twelfth Cakes.

Take an ounce of cochineal beat very fine; add three gills of water, a quarter of an ounce of roche-alum, and two ounces of lump sugar; boil them together for twenty minutes, strain it through a fine sieve, and preserve it for use close covered.

Twelfth Cakes.

Take seven pounds of flour, make a cavity in the center, set a sponge with a gill and a half of yest and a little warm milk; then put round it one pound of fresh butter broke into small lumps, one pound and a quarter of sifted sugar, four pounds and a half of currants washed and picked, half an ounce of sifted cinnamon, a quarter of an ounce of pounded cloves, mace, and nutmeg mixed, sliced candied orange or lemon peel and citron. When the sponge is risen mix all the ingredients together with a little warm milk; let the hoops be well papered and buttered, then fill them with the mixture and bake them, and when nearly cold ice them over with sugar prepared for that purpose as per receipt; or they may be plain.

Bristol Cakes.

Take six ounces of sifted sugar, six ounces of fresh butter, four whites and two yolks of eggs, nine ounces of flour, and mix them well together in an earthen pan with the hand; then add three quarters of a pound of picked currants, and drop the mixture with a spoon upon tin plates rubbed with butter, and bake them in a brisk oven.

Hyde Park Corner Cakes.

Take two pounds of flour, four ounces of common sugar, and half an ounce of carraway seeds pounded; then set a sponge with half a gill of yest and some warm milk, and when it works take some boiling milk, add to it five ounces of fresh butter, mix it up light, add let it lay some time; then roll it out, cut it into what forms you please, and bake them in a moderate oven.

Good Gingerbread Nuts.

Take four pounds of flour, half a pound of sifted sugar, one ounce of carraway seeds, half an ounce of ginger pounded and sifted, six ounces of fresh butter, and two ounces of candied orange peel cut into small slices. Then take a pound of treacle or honey and a gill of cream, make them warm together, mix all the ingredients into a paste, and let it lay six hours; then roll it out, make it into nuts, and bake them in a moderate oven.

Bride Cake.

Take two pounds of sifted loaf sugar, four pounds of fresh butter, four pounds of best white flour dried and sifted, a quarter of an ounce of mace and cinnamon, likewise the same quantity of nutmeg pounded and sifted, thirty eggs, four pounds of currants washed, picked, and dried before a fire, a pound of jordan almonds blanched and pounded, a pound of citron, a pound of candied orange and a pound of candied lemon peels cut into slices, and half a pint of brandy; then proceed as follows:—First work the butter to a cream with the hand, then beat in the sugar for a quarter of an hour, whisk the whites of eggs to a solid froth, and mix them with the sugar and butter; then beat the yolks for a quarter of an hour and put them to the above, likewise add the flour, mace, and nutmeg; beat all well together till the oven is ready, and then mix in lightly the brandy, currants, almonds, and sweetmeats. Line a hoop with paper, rub it with butter, fill it with the mixture, bake it in a brisk oven, and when it is risen cover it with paper to prevent it from burning. It may be served up either iced or plain.

Rice Cakes.

Whisk the yolks of seven eggs for a quarter of an hour, add five ounces of sifted sugar, and mix them well; put to them a quarter of a pound of rice, some flour, a little brandy, the rind of a lemon grated very fine, and a small quantity of pounded mace; then beat six whites of eggs for some time, mix all together for ten minutes, fill a hoop with the mixture, and bake it in a brisk oven.

Bath Cakes.

Take a pound of fresh butter and rub with it a pound of flour, mix them into a light paste with a gill of yest and some warm cream, and set it in a warm place to rise; then mould in with it a few carraway seeds, make it into cakes the size of small french rolls, and bake them on tins buttered.

Pancakes.

To half a pound of best white flour sifted add a little salt, grated nutmeg, cream or new milk, and mix them well together; then whisk eight eggs, put them to the above, and beat the mixture for ten minutes till perfectly smooth and light, and let it be of a moderate thickness. When the cakes are to be fried, put a little piece of lard or fresh butter in each frying-pan over a regular fire, and when hot put in the mixture, a sufficient quantity just to cover the bottom of each pan, fry them of a nice colour, and serve them up very hot. Serve with them, likewise, some sifted loaf sugar, pounded cinnamon, and seville orange, on separate plates.

N. B. Before the frying pans are used let them be prepared with a bit of butter put into each and burnt; then wipe them very clean with a dry cloth, as this method prevents the batter from sticking to the pan when frying.

Shrewsbury Cakes.

Beat half a pound of fresh butter to a cream, add to it the same quantity of flour, one egg, six ounces of sifted sugar, and a quarter of an ounce of carraway seeds. Mix all together into a paste, roll it out thin, stamp it with a tin cutter, prick the cakes with a fork, lay them on tin plates rubbed with butter, and bake them in a slow oven.

Portugal Cakes, or Heart Cakes.

TAKE a pound of flour, a pound of sifted sugar, a pound of fresh butter, and mix them with the hand (or a whisk) till they become like a fine batter. Then add two spoonfuls of rose water, half a pound of currants washed and picked, break ten eggs, whisk them, and mix well all together. Butter ten moulds, fill them three parts full with the mixture, and bake them in a brisk oven.

Macaroons.

TAKE a pound of jordan almonds blanched and pounded fine, with a little rose water to preserve them from oiling, and add a pound of sifted sugar; then whisk the whites of ten eggs to a solid froth and add to the above; beat all together for some time. Have ready wafer paper on tin plates, drop the mixture over it separately the size of a shilling or smaller, sift a little sugar over, and bake them.

Mirangles.

TAKE the whites of nine eggs, and whisk them to a solid froth; then add the rind of six lemons grated very fine and a spoonful of sifted sugar; after which lay a wet sheet of paper on a tin, and with a spoon drop the mixture in little lumps separately upon it, sift sugar over, and bake them in a moderately heated oven, observing they are of a nice colour. Then put raspberry, apricot, or any other kind of jam between two bottoms, add them together, and lay them in a warm place or before the fire to dry.

Ratafias.

BLANCH and pound half a pound of jordan almonds, likewise the same quantity of bitter almonds, and preserve them from oiling with rose water; then add a pound of sifted sugar, beat the whites of four eggs well, and mix lightly with them; after which put the mixture into a preserving pan, set it over a moderate fire, stirring till it is pretty hot, and when it is cold roll it into small rolls, cut them into small cakes the bigness of a shilling, dip the top of your finger into flour and touch lightly each cake, put them on wafer paper, sift sugar over, and bake them in a slow oven.

Lemon Puffs.

PUT a pound of sifted loaf sugar in a bowl with the juice of two lemons, and beat them together; then whisk the white of an egg to a very high froth, add it to the mixture, and whisk it for twenty minutes; after which put to it the rind of three lemons grated very fine and three eggs, mixing all well together. Sift sugar over wafer paper, drop on it the mixture in small quantities, and bake them in a moderately heated oven.

Chantilly Basket.

HAVE ready a small quantity of warm clarified sugar boiled to a carmel height, dip ratafia cakes into it, and place them round the inside of a dish. Then cut more ratafia cakes into squares, dip them into the sugar, pile them on the others, and so on for two or three stories high. After which line the inside with wafer paper, fill with sponge biscuits, sweetmeats, blanched almonds, and some made cream as for an apple pie, put some trifle froth over that, and garnish the froth with rose leaves, or coloured comfits or carmel of sugar thrown lightly over the top.

Green Codlins, frosted with Sugar.

TAKE twelve codlins, blanch them in water with a little roche-alum in it and some vine leaves; when they are nearly done take off the outside skin, rub the apples over with oiled fresh butter, and sift plenty of sugar over them; then lay them on a clean tin, put them into a slow oven, and when the sugar sparkles like frost take them out. When they are cold serve them up in a trifle glass with some perfumed cream round them made as for an apple pie, and on the top of each codlin stick a small flower for garnish.

Pound Cake.

TAKE a pound of sifted sugar, a pound of fresh butter, and mix them with the hand for ten minutes; then put to them nine yolks and five whites of eggs beaten, whisk them well, and add a pound of sifted flour, a few carraway seeds, a quarter of a pound of candied orange peel cut into slices, a few currants washed and picked, and mix all together as light as possible.

Yest Cake.

TAKE one pound of flour, two pounds of currants washed and picked, a quarter of a pound of fresh butter, a quarter of a pound of lisbon sugar, a quarter of a pound of citron and candied orange peel cut into slices, cinnamon and mace a small quantity of each pounded and sifted. Make a cavity in the center of the ingredients, add a gill of sweet wine, a little warm milk, a teacupful of yest, and let it stand till the yest works; then put a little more warm milk, mix all together, fill a hoop with it, and let it remain till risen, and bake it.

Rich Plum Cake.

TAKE one pound of sifted sugar, one pound of fresh butter, and mix them with the hand in a earthen dish for a quarter of an hour. Then beat well ten yolks and five whites of eggs, put two thirds of them to the sugar and butter, and mix them together till it begins to be tough; after which add one pound and a half of currants washed and picked, a quarter of a pound of citron, a quarter of a pound of candied orange or lemon peel cut into slices, a quarter of a pound of jordan almonds blanched and bruised very fine. Then pound a quarter of a pound of muscadine raisins, put to them a gill of sweet wine and a spoonful of brandy, strain the liquor through a cloth to the mixture, add the rest of the eggs, and mix all together as light as possible.

Dried Cherries.

GATHER the largest flemish cherries (or english bearers) when nearly ripe, pick off the stalks and take the stones away; have ready a thin syrup boiling-hot, put the cherries into it, and let them remain till the next day; then strain and boil the liquor again, and add to the cherries; the same again on the third day; on the fourth day strain the syrup, add more sugar, and clarify it; boil it to a strong consistence, add the cherries, put them into jars, and when they are cold cover them close. When wanted for use take them out, lay them on large drying sieves, and put them in a very slack oven.

N. B. In the same manner may be done apricots, pears, plums, &c.

Pippins with Rice.

BOIL two ounces of whole rice with half a pint of milk, and when it is nearly absorbed put the rice into a marble mortar, add a table spoonful of brandy, a little grated lemon peel, a small quantity of pounded cinnamon and cloves, two ounces of sifted sugar, two eggs, and pound all together. Then pare twelve large ripe golden pippins, core them with an apple scoop, mould over them some of the mixture with the hand, put writing paper on a tin-plate, rub it over with sweet oil or butter, put the apples on it, and bake them gently till done; then serve them up in a deep dish with melted butter over and a little of the syrup of quinces mixed with it.

To make English Bread.

TAKE a peck of the best white flour, sift it into a trough, make a cavity in the center, and strain through a hair sieve (mixed together) a pint of good yest and a pint of lukewarm water; mix them lightly with some of the flour till of a light paste, set it in a warm place covered over to prove for an hour; then mix the whole with two quarts of lukewarm water and a little salt, knead it, let it be of a good stiffness, prove it an hour more and knead it again; prove it another hour, mould it into loaves or batch two pieces together, and bake them in a brisk oven.

N. B. A middling-size loaf will require an hour and a half in baking.

French Bread.

SIFT a peck of fine flour into a trough, make a cavity in the center with the hand, strain into it (mixed together) a pint of lukewarm milk and a pint of good yest; mix them with some of the flour till of a light sponge, set it in a warm place covered over to prove for an hour; then add to it two quarts of lukewarm milk, half a pound of fresh butter, an ounce of sifted loaf sugar, and a little salt; knead it till of a nice stiffness, let it prove an hour more, knead it again, and let it prove another hour; then mould it into bricks, lay them on tins, put them into a very slack oven or warm place to prove for half an hour, and bake them in a brisk oven.

Pulpton of Apples.

PARE, cut into quarters, and core eight good-sized baking apples; put them into a stewpan, add a bit of lemon peel and a table spoonful of rose water; cover the pan close, put it over a slow fire, and when the apples are tender rub them through a hair sieve, put to the pulp, sugar to the palate, sifted cinnamon and cloves a small quantity of each, four eggs well beaten, a quarter of a pound of the crumb of french bread soaked in a gill of cream, and mix all the ingredients together. Rub the inside of a mould with fresh butter, fill it with the mixture, bake it in a moderately heated oven, when done turn it out on a dish, and serve it up with sifted sugar over.

A sweet Omlet of Eggs.

MIX well together ten eggs, half a gill of cream, a quarter of a pound of oiled fresh butter and a little syrup of nutmeg; sweeten it with loaf sugar, put the mixture into a prepared frying pan as for a savory omlet, fry it in the same manner, and serve it up with a little sifted sugar over it.

To keep Cucumbers for Winter Use for Sauces.

TAKE fresh gathered middling-sized cucumbers, put them into a jar, have ready half vinegar, half water, and some salt, a sufficient quantity to cover them; make it boiling-hot, pour it over them, add sweet oil, cover the jars down close with bladder and leather, and set them in a dry place.

To preserve Mushrooms for Sauces.

PEEL button forced mushrooms, wash them and boil till half done in a sufficient quantity of salt and water to cover them; then drain them and dry in the sun, boil the liquor with different spices, put the mushrooms into a jar, pour the boiling pickle over them, add sweet oil, and tie them over with bladder, &c.

Pullet roasted with Batter.

BONE and force the pullet with good stuffing or forcemeat, paper it and put it to roast; when half done take off the paper, and baste the fowl with a little light batter; let it dry, baste it again, so repeating till it is done and nicely crusted over; then serve it up with benshamelle or poivrade sauce beneath.

Dutch Beef.

RUB the prime ribs of fat beef with common salt, and let them lay in a pan for three days; then rub them with the different articles as for hams or tongues, and add plenty of bruised juniper berries. Turn the meat every two days for three weeks, and smoke it.

Mushroom Ketchup.

TAKE a parcel of mushrooms either natural or forced, the latter will prove the best, and cut off part of the stalk towards the root. Wash the mushrooms clean, drain them, then bruise them a little in a marble mortar, put them into an earthen vessel with a middling quantity of salt, let them remain for four days, and then strain them through a tamis cloth. When the sediment is settled pour the liquor into a stewpan, and to every pint of juice add half a gill of red port, a little whole allspice, cloves, mace, and pepper. Boil them together twenty minutes, then skim and strain the ketchup, and when cold put it into small bottles and cork them close.

Suet Pudding.

CHOP fine half a pound of beef suet, add to it the same quantity of flour, two eggs beaten, a little salt, a small quantity of pounded and sifted ginger, and mix them together with milk. Let the mixture be of a moderate thickness. It may be either boiled or baked.

Savoy Cake.

BEAT well together the yolks of eight eggs and a pound of sifted sugar, and whisk the whites till of a solid froth; then take six ounces of flour and a little sifted cinnamon, and mix all the ingredients lightly together; after which rub a mould with fresh butter, fill it three parts full with the mixture, and bake it in a slack heated oven.

Nutmeg Syrup.

POUND a quarter of a pound of nutmegs, put them into a stewpan, add a pint and a half of hot water, and boil them for half an hour; then strain, and put to a pint of liquor two pounds of sifted sugar and one egg beat up with a little cold water; set it over a fire, and when it boils skim it till perfectly clear and reduced to a good syrup, and when it is cold mix with it half a pint of brandy.

Having this syrup always at hand will answer a better purpose for puddings, &c. than grated nutmeg and brandy, as the mixtures can be better palated, and likewise save trouble and expense.

Sweetbreads with Veal and Ham.

BLANCH heart sweetbreads eight minutes, and wash and wipe them dry; then make an incision in the under part, take out a piece and pound it with a small quantity of light forcemeat; after which fill the cavity in the sweetbread, rub the top with white of egg, lay over it a thin slice of lean ham, a slice of veal, and a bard of bacon; put paper and a thin sheet of common paste over the whole, bake them gently for an hour, and when they are to be served up take off the paste and paper, glaize lightly the bacon, and put under the sweetbreads a good benshamelle.

Essence of Ham for Sauces.

TAKE four pounds of slices of lean ham, and be careful it is of a good flavour; put it into a stewpan with a little water, six peeled eschallots, and two bay leaves;

cover the pan close, set it over a fire, and simmer the ham till three parts done; then add two quarts of water and boil it till tender, strain it through a fine sieve, skim it perfectly free from fat, clear it with whites of eggs, strain it through a tamis, boil it till it is reduced to a pint, and when cold put it into small bottles and cork them close.

Ox Heart roasted.

LET the heart be very fresh, wash and wipe it, fill it with a stuffing as for a fillet of veal, tie over the top a piece of veal caul, roast it gently one hour and an half, and five minutes before it is done roast it quick, froth it with flour and butter, and put it on a very hot dish. Serve it up with a sauce under it made with cullis, fresh butter, a table spoonful of ketchup, and half a gill of red port boiled together.

Slices of Cod fried with Oysters.

EGG, breadcrumb, and fry in boiling lard, some slices of crimped cod; when done, drain them dry, serve them up with oyster sauce in the center, made in the same manner as for beef steaks.

Small Crusts to be eaten with Cheese or Wine after Dinner.

TAKE the crumb of a new-baked loaf, pull it into small pieces, put them on a baking plate, and set them in a moderately heated oven till they are of a nice brown colour.

Devilled Almonds.

BLANCH half a pound of jordan almonds and wipe them dry; then put into a frying-pan two ounces of fresh butter, make it hot, add the almonds, fry them gently till of a good brown colour, drain them on a hair sieve, strew over cayenne pepper and some salt, and serve them up hot.

Boiled Tripe and Onions.

CUT a prepared double of tripe into slips, then peel and boil some spanish or other onions in milk and water with a little salt, and when they are nearly done add the tripe and boil it gently ten minutes. Serve it to table with the onions and a little of the liquor in a tureen. Serve up, likewise, in a sauceboat, some melted butter with a little mustard mixed with it, and (if approved) there may be added a table spoonful of vinegar.

Boiled Sweetbreads.

BLANCH two heart sweetbreads, wash and trim off the pipe, then boil them in milk and water with a little salt for half an hour; drain them dry, and when they are to be served to table put over them some boiling benshamelle with a little parsley chopped very fine in it.

Broiled Sweetbreads.

BLANCH the sweetbreads till half done, wash and trim off the pipe, then cut them into large slices, season with a small quantity of cayenne pepper and salt, broil them gently over a clear fire till of a nice brown colour, and serve them up very hot, with some cold fresh butter on a plate.

Conclusion, with Remarks.

ALL sweets, pastry, shellfish or savoury dishes, either plain or modelled, with fat or butter, or ornaments of any kind, that are served up in second courses or ball suppers, &c. should be very light, airy, and neat; the pastry, likewise, of the best puff paste, well-baked, and rather inclining to a pale colour, which has a very good effect.

Let it also be observed, that mention should have been made in the receipt for Mock Turtle, of an addition to the passing of flour and butter, to each gallon of liquor half a pint of madeira wine; and (if approved) the mock turtle may be made with pieces of cow-heel or pig's head instead of calf's scalp.

THE END.

H

I

J

L

M

Q

R

Lector House believes that a society develops through a two-fold approach of continuous learning and adaptation, which is derived from the study of classic literary works spread across the historic timeline of literature records. Therefore, we aim at reviving, repairing and redeveloping all those inaccessible or damaged but historically as well as culturally important literature across subjects so that the future generations may have an opportunity to study and learn from past works to embark upon a journey of creating a better future.

This book is a result of an effort made by Lector House towards making a contribution to the preservation and repair of original ancient works which might hold historical significance to the approach of continuous learning across subjects.

HAPPY READING & LEARNING!

LECTOR HOUSE LLP
E-MAIL: lectorpublishing@gmail.com

9 789389 614022